Beach Freaks'

Guide to Michigan's Best Beaches

by

Joan and Bob Elmouchi

GLOVEBOX
GUIDEBOOKS
OF AMERICA
1112 Washburn Place East
Saginaw, MI 48602-2977

Travel outdoors entails some unavoidable risks. Know your limitations, be prepared, be alert, use good judgement, think safety and enjoy Michigan's great beaches.

Interior design by Dan Jacalone
Cover and interior photos: Bob Elmouchi
Senior Editor, William P. Cornish
Managing Editor, Penny Weber-Bailey

Published by: **Glovebox Guidebooks of America**
1112 Washburn Place East
Saginaw, Michigan 48602-2977
orders: (800) 289-4843 or (517) 792-8363

Library of Congress, CIP.
Elmouchi, Joan, 1952-
Elmouchi, Bob, 1951-

Beach Freaks'
Guide to Michigan's Best Beaches
(A Glovebox Guidebooks of America publication)
ISBN 1-881139-23-9

Printed in the United States of America

10 9 8 7 6 5 4 3 2 1

Dedicated to our families, for their unwavering love and support

CONTENTS

Introduction

One thing we can say for certain - beaches are always changing. Varying lake levels create beaches and erode them, winds can alter the shape of a shoreline, dunes are constantly shifting.

People change things, too. Facilities get added and upgraded, a concession stand can close or an entrance fee can alter. Our reviews are based on what we found when we visited beaches over the course of three summers. Some beaches, such as the one at Orchard Beach State Park, were so eroded that we couldn't include them in this book. The beach you find during your visit may not look exactly the same as when it was reviewed.

Our comments are obviously subjective, and there's no doubt that a beach visited on a sunny, warm day may have been more favorably viewed than one we had to review in an overcast chill. We did, however, attempt to measure all the sites using the same criteria for sand, water, view, atmosphere and amenities. The beach sizes mentioned in the book are primarily estimates. They are included to give the reader an idea of the length and depth of a beach and are not intended to be exact measurements.

We'd like to thank the many park rangers, lifeguards, DNR staff and local residents who answered our questions and gave us the inside scoop on the lovely beaches that we had the pleasure of visiting. It's been a labor of love and the best job a couple of beach freaks could hope to have.

DIRECTIONS AND MAPS

We provide a narrative with directions to each beach. Most often we will direct you beginning from the nearest city or highway. Whenever possible we try to keep on paved roads, but even the dirt roads we traveled were in good enough condition to be negotiated with a compact sedan. A four-wheel drive or sport utility vehicle is not needed to get to any of these beaches.

For cross-state trips we used maps provided by AAA of Michigan. State maps are also available through gas stations and book stores. We also relied on two excellent atlases, the Michigan Atlas & Gazetteer by DeLorme and the Michigan County Atlas by Universal Map.

Each of these atlases has its advantages and disadvantages. The Michigan Atlas & Gazetteer breaks up the state into 101 rectangular sections, whereas the Michigan County Atlas divides the state by each of its 83 counties. Every once in a while we found that the beach we were driving to sits either in the crease of the spine or right on the edge of the map. Because each atlas illustrates the state differently, if this was a problem we would just switch to the other atlas. The atlases also contain special features such as golf course, camping and waterfall listings, county information and mileage tables. The DeLorme does a better job of representing the Upper Peninsula while the Universal noted a few more of the beaches in our book. I wouldn't worry much about which atlas to buy, but we do suggest that you purchase one of them. You can find them at most book stores and gas station mini-marts.

To make it easier for you to find your desired beach, we have provided a "beach finder" with each review that lists the page (or map) number and coordinates for each atlas. We also recommend that you purchase an inexpensive compass. It's easy to get turned around on an overcast day and many of our directions use compass headings.

Also keep in mind that both of these atlases contain some errors. Sometimes they give a wrong street name or show a beach in the wrong location. Some of the most beautiful beaches we reviewed cannot be found in either atlas and are truly "off the beaten path."

TRAVEL SITES ON THE INTERNET

The Internet and the World Wide Web have made planning a Michigan vacation easier than ever. The following general sites provide a wealth of information on lodging, camping, attractions, restaurants and more:

The Michigan Travel Companion
www.yesmichigan.com

Michigan Recreation Channel from RING!online
www.ring.com/mitravel.htm

Michigan Travel Bureau, Travel Michigan
www. michigan.org

Running Creek's Michigan Traveler's Guide
www. running-creek/com/Michigan

AAA Travel Online
www.aamich.com

West Michigan Tourist Association
www.wmta.org

The following specialized sites provide comprehensive information on specific topics:

Michigan State Parks
www.dnr.state.mi.us.www/parks

Michigan Wilderness Areas, Great Outdoors Recreation Pages
www. gorp.com/gorp/resource/US_Wilderness_Area/mi.htm

Michigan Campground Directory
www.michcampgrounds.com

Michigan Lake to Lake Bed and Breakfast Association
www.laketolake.com

Michigan State Forest Campgrounds and Pathways
www.dnr.state.mi.us/www/fmd/rec/location.htm

Cities throughout Michigan now offer home pages on the world wide web. Most can be accessed by typing in the name of the city followed by .com, such as www.petoskey.com, www.tawas.com, and www.saugatuck.com. These sites offer valuable information on area attractions, festivals, lodgings, restaurants and more.

The Beachfreak Commandments

1. If you brought it with you, take it when you leave. The only thing you should leave behind is your footprints. The beach is a very delicate ecosystem. None of the animals that live at the beach consume plastic bags, tin foil or cigarette butts, and your trash may be harmful to birds or fish. Please keep in mind that if you leave trash on the beach, you will diminish the very quality that drew you there.

2. Stay off protected dune areas. Dune life is so fragile that even a footprint can damage emerging dune plants.

3. Bring no noisemakers. Let yourself and others enjoy the soothing sounds of nature. Use a Walkman and headphones rather than imposing your music on others. Leave the whistling football and drum-like Ping-Pong paddles at home. If you really can't have fun without making noise, then make sure that you are far enough away that nobody else can hear you over the gentle sound of the surf.

4. Don't feed the seagulls. They get aggressive, they swarm, and you don't want the end results of your feeding landing on your head.

5. Watch your children, especially at unguarded beaches.

6. If park rules say "No Pets," don't bring your dog to the beach. If dogs are allowed, keep them on a leash. Clean up after your dog, and if Fido is afraid of the water, don't force him into the lake!

7. Use sunscreen. The sun is a constant nuclear explosion happening 98 million miles away, and you need to take precautions when exposing yourself to solar radiation. Be especially careful to protect the sensitive skin of babies and children.

8. Be courteous. Have fun in the water but don't splash or roughhouse near other bathers. Avoid shaking out your towel where the wind will blow sand on your neighbor. Don't throw sand or play sports in a crowded area.

9. Don't stare directly at the sun, even at sunset. It can permanently damage your eyes.

10. Enjoy!

The Zen of Beachfreaking

Bored to death with repetitious jogging on concrete and asphalt? Seeking a universe whose limits are greater than the four walls of your office? Looking for a place where you can see the horizon? Then make a change... take a chance. Go to a place you've never been before. Get toasty-warm under the sun. Spend hours laying on silky smooth sand. Let the day drift by as you lose yourself to the rhythmic sound of rolling waves. Become mesmerized by sparkling sunlight dancing on crystal-blue water. Feel sand that's so clean it squeaks under your toes as you shuffle along the shoreline. Watch a glowing orange orb slowly disappear as it sets upon iridescent waves awash with lavender, purple and blue. These are just a few of countless pleasurable moments we've experienced on Michigan's beaches, enjoyable moments shared by people visiting Michigan beaches every summer.

Spending a day at the beach will create memories to last a lifetime. The beach is an ideal place for retreat and contemplation, somewhere to get away from the everyday stresses of life and get back in touch with nature. Experience the openness, the expanse and the overpowering natural beauty of a Michigan beach.

MICHIGAN'S SAND DUNES

Tourism is big business in Michigan, second only in revenue to the automobile industry. In 1997 Michigan ranked sixth in the nation as a vacation destination; among the Midwestern states it took top honors. Not all of those visitors were from out of state. In fact, nearly 2/3 of the 34 million trips taken in 1997 were from Michiganders making their own state their travel destination.

Michigan residents are proud of the natural wonders their state has to offer. They are especially proud of Michigan's sand dunes, 270 miles representing the highest and longest system of fresh water dunes in the world. A stunningly beautiful and valuable resource, it took a unique set of circumstances to create the beaches and dunes of Michigan.

IN THE BEGINNING

The story begins with thousands of years of snow crystallization that formed the continental glaciers. These glaciers, fed by cold and snow, slowly began to move south from the arctic until they eventually covered the Great Lakes area with mile-thick masses of ice. Their movement averaged only a few thousand feet a year, trapping rocks and soil as they went. It may have taken 4,000 years for a rock from the Arctic to reach the Great Lakes area. These massive glaciers also carved huge depressions into the river valleys that eventually filled with meltwaters, creating the Great Lakes.

Climactic changes and global warming eventually caused the glaciers to retreat. There were many periods of retreat and advance before the glaciers made their final departure from the Great Lake's area. Glaciers resculpted Michigan's landscape for between 500,000 and two million years before their final withdrawal over 10,000 years ago, and each time a glacier's movement changed it discharged rock, gravel, sand and clay into mounds called moraines. The forces of wind and water in combination with the moraines formed the Great Lakes sand dunes. It was the ancient forces of the glaciers, the huge bodies of water left by their melting, the pulverized rock they left behind and the powerful forces of wind and waves that combined to produce the phenomena of the dunes.

GREAT LAKES SAND

Tiny quartz crystals combine to produce Michigan's silky sand, a substance so fine that shuffling your feet often produces "singing sand". This musical sound is recognized on beaches all over the world and has been documented from as early as 800 AD China. This phenomenon is called "singing sand" on small beaches, "booming sand" in the desert, and "barking sand" on Hawaii's calcium carbonate sea-shell beaches.

The glaciers' gift of quartz-bearing rocks such as granite and sandstone were pounded and pulverized by the waves of the ancient Great Lakes, which carried the quartz into the lakes as sand. Inland, rivers formed from the melting glaciers carried more sand and pebbles toward the newly formed lakes. The sand then became part of the lake bottom which eventually was exposed by the movement of wind and water, creating a beach.

Wave action deposits sand granules from the lake bottom onto the beach. Once deposited, the water binds the granules together until the wind dries and sorts them. Heavier grains will stay on the beach, while finer grains will blow away in a breeze as light as eight miles an hour. Sand grains on the Great Lakes beaches are fairly consistent in size and shape, with 80% of granules being ¼ to ½ millimeter in size. It is the abrasive action of the wind blowing over the sand, and the sand whipping against the rocks that shapes each grain.

FORMATION OF THE DUNES

How are new dunes formed? Two types of dunes can be found on Michigan's shoreline. Low-lying beach dunes are created from beach sand. Winds blowing inland from the Great Lakes carrying grains of sand slow when meeting a barrier. The sand falls, landing on a rock or a mound of dirt. The more the wind blows, the more the sand travels and falls, slowly building into a gently graded incline. When the height of the sandy mound reaches between three and ten feet it is considered a dune. The high dunes, such as the Sleeping Bear, are called perched dunes. These dunes sit above the shore on plateaus and were formed from glacial moraines.

The dunes closest to the lake are called foredunes. These are the most recently formed dunes and are usually between thirty to fifty feet in height. Excellent examples of foredunes can be seen at Sleeping Bear Dunes and Silver Lake State Park. As these dunes face the lake and bear the unprotected force of storms they are frequently damaged by waves and wind. Behind the foredunes may be older, higher dunes that can cover thousands of acres, are covered by forests and are no longer recognizable as dunes at all.

How and when a Great Lakes dune will grow or move depends primarily on three forces: the land itself, water, and plant life. Wind loses velocity very quickly as it crosses over land. Without strength the wind cannot carry the sand, therefore dune growth and movement occur only in an area within ½ mile of the shoreline. Rainfall and groundwater determine how far dunes will move and how much land mass they will cover. Water affects plant life, and as plant life increases on a dune the less vulnerable it is to wind. Additionally, plants capture airborne grains of sand and help the dune to grow. Dunes also need sand to grow — the wider the beach, the greater the potential for large dunes to form.

Essential to the formation and stabilization of the dunes are the dune grasses. These grasses retain moisture and provide shade which moderate the daytime temperatures and create a less hostile environment for other plants to take hold. One of the first of these grasses is marram grass, or American beach grass. This essential plant flourishes under the harsh conditions of barren dunes. It forms new plants through rhizomes, underground stems that grow outward from the main plant, sending new roots down to find water and new shoots upwards to form new plants. These fine, hair-like roots can spread over a twenty foot area trapping water and nutrients. Marram grass also has the ability to elongate its stem, allowing the plant to survive sand burial of up to three feet a year.

Another plant early on the scene is sand reed grass, which has shorter rhizome and survives in areas where the wind is less intense or erosion is slower. Cottonwood trees and sand cherry may also be spotted early in dune development. Cottonwoods can survive sand burial, grow aggressively and have roots that may travel as far as one hundred feet down seeking moisture. Fragile dune plants are easily damaged, which is why visitors are urged to stay on marked paths and stairways. When plants disappear, dunes become vulnerable to high winds and bowl-shaped blow-outs may occur.

DUNE PRESERVATION

The natural forces that combined thousands of years ago to create the dunes will probably never be repeated. Sand dunes are fragile structures, made up of an unconsolidated, cohesionless material that is very susceptible to erosion. Damage or removal of a dune's vegetative cover can lead to significant damage by creating open areas that are vulnerable to the forces of wind and water.

In 1976 Michigan's Governor Milliken signed the Sand Dune Protection and Management Act that regulated sand mining. But condominium and housing development continued to pose a threat as dunes were leveled, so in 1985 the Department of Natural Resources established a new sand dunes program which identified 70,000 acres as "critical dune areas" requiring protection. In 1989 Governor Blanchard amended the act, requiring a permit from the Department of Environmental Quality for any development occurring in regulated dune areas.

New standards included in the amendments offered substantial protection for dune areas. Further revisions made the requirements even stricter, and now the DEQ ensures that all development is compatible with the sensitive features of the sand dune system. For more information on the preservation of Great Lakes sand dunes, contact the DEQ, Land and Water Management Division, Box 30458, Lansing Michigan 48909.

Key to Symbols

Lifeguard

Restrooms - If the only available restrooms are out-houses, it will be noted in the text.

Changing Rooms

Showers - The shower symbol denotes either a full indoor shower or an outdoor rinse-off shower. Some showers may be coin operated.

Water Fountain

Beverage Machine

Picnic Tables

Barbecue Grills

Concession Stand

Pay Telephone

Play Area

Volleyball

Boat Launch

Camping

Handicapped Accessible - This symbol denotes beaches with accessible facilities such as restrooms, but does not necessarily indicate wheelchair access to the beach itself.

The unique mix of Michigan's golden sugar and black magnatite sands are sculpted by the hands of the Great Lakes.

BEST OF THE BEACHES

BEACH FREAK'S TOP TEN

1. Wilderness State Park, Sturgeon Bay Beach, city of Carp Lake
2. Michigan Recreation Area, Manistee National Forest, Manistee
3. Fisherman's Island State Park, Charlevoix
4. Ludington State Park, Ludington
5. North Bar Lake Nature Preserve, Empire
6. Warren Dunes State Park, Sawyer
7. Silver Lake State Park, Little Sable Point Lighthouse Beach, Mears
8. Lake Township Park and Platte River Point, Lake Township
9. Cheboygan State Park, Cheboygan
10. Tunnel Park, Holland

HONORABLE MENTION

1. Tawas Point State Park, East Tawas
2. Duck Lake State Park, Whitehall
3. Kirk Park, West Olive
4. Esch Road Beach, Empire
5. Metro Beach Metropark, Mt. Clemens

Wilderness State Park, Sturgeon Bay Beach.

Addison Oaks County Park.

1 Addison Oaks County Park

Addison Oaks County Park is one of those places where the quality of the experience depends on the size of the crowd. A small crowd finds a charming beach, a delightful swimming hole and first-rate facilities. A busy weekend during the peak summer months, however, may turn the compact swimming area into rush hour at the watering hole.

The southwest corner of Buhl Lake forms a cove which makes up the swimming beach. A 150-foot long by 50-foot wide sandy beach wraps around the cove. The beach is attractive but small, bisected by a picturesque pine. The sand is relatively soft but contains a high dirt content. The roped swimming area is quite small and can quickly get crowded.

Floats are allowed in the section nearest the shore. A deeper section with a wooden platform is for swimmers only, and quickly fills up with older kids and teenagers. Despite the coziness of the swimming area, three lifeguard stands are staffed. Two aerating fountains keep the water moving, and the lake quality is monitored twice a week for bacterial growth that may be caused by birds or other animal life. Algae growth is controlled by a spraying program.

A spacious lawn leads to the beach from an unpaved parking lot. There are two large rental pavilions available, as well as tented shelters which are set up in the summer. Offered on the shady lawn are an abundance of tables and grills as well as three sand volleyball courts and an 18 hole disc golf course. The concession building also houses a video game room and an outdoor deck with a view of the lake. All of the park's outbuildings are designed in a Swiss chalet style that blend attractively with their wooded surroundings.

The children's area is impressive, with a nifty wooden play structure that incorporates bridges, slides, and climbing devices. This well-maintained park has plenty of room to spread out, but can get congested around the beach and swimming area. Because the day use area encompasses only a corner of Buhl Lake, the beaching experience is more that of a pond than of a large inland lake.

ABOUT THE PARK: This pleasant park in northern Oakland County has much to offer. Modern, semi-modern and primitive campsites as well as group and youth camping are available, as are rental cabins. Mountain biking is extremely popular, and five bike trails of varying difficulty are located throughout the west side of the park. The east side of the park has hiking trails from a fifth of a mile to almost two miles in length. Mountain bikes can be rented, as can rowboats and pedal boats for a cruise on quiet Buhl Lake (which does not allow motor boats).

Fishing in Buhl Lake and smaller Adams Lake is also a popular pastime, and fishing rods are available for rental. Addison Oaks is a sought-after spot for weddings which are booked into the modern conference center and gardens.

In winter, 12 miles of groomed ski trails, ski rentals, and a lighted 1.5-mile trail are provided. Ice fishing and ice skating are also activities in the park, and special events such as hayrides, fishing tournaments, mountain bike races and learn to ski days take place throughout the year.

FEES: Oakland County Resident: $5 a day, $25 annual. Non-resident: $8 a day, $45 annual. $2 senior citizens weekdays

DIRECTIONS: From M-59, take the Rochester Road exit to Rochester Road (M-150). Go north on Rochester Road approximately 12 miles to Romeo Road. Head left on Romeo Road for

BEACH FINDER

PARK NAME	DELORME	UNIVERSAL
Addison Oaks County Park	pg. 42, B1	map 63, J1

two miles to the park entrance.

FURTHER INFORMATION: Addison Oaks County Park, 1480 W. Romeo Rd., Leonard MI (810) 693-2432

2 Bald Mountain Recreation Area

There are 11 lakes at the Bald Mountain Recreation Area, but only one swimming beach bordered by a hill covered with scruffy grass. Located at the south side of the park's largest body of water, Lower Trout Lake, the 400-yard by 60-foot sandy area is spacious enough to handle a summer crowd.

The beach fronts a hilly picnic area strewn with tables, grills and two sets of play equipment. The sand is dark and coarse but is free of large pebbles and stones. The view is typical for an inland lake, a close horizon of deciduous trees plus a northern facing beach which tends to aim you away from the sunset. The lake slopes gently down to a depth of only four or five feet, and the buoyed swimming area is generous. The relatively clear water allows a view of the yellow/green sand below and of minnows darting around your legs.

There is no mountain at Bald Mountain - it was bulldozed into a landfill. The recreation area is made up of three distinct units. The south unit offers a shooting range, which provides opportunities for shooting skeet, trap, archery, rifles and handguns. The northern unit is loaded with lakes, many of which have fishing access and boat launches. Both units contain trails - 15 miles of hiking and mountain biking trails and eight miles of cross-country ski trails. The western unit consists of undeveloped farmland. There is no campground, but two rustic cabins are available to rent.

ABOUT THE PARK: Bald Mountain is a fisherman's paradise.

Bass, bluegills and crappies abound in the lakes, and fly fishermen can try for trout in the two creeks at the park's southern end. Snow makes winter a busy season as the park offers groomed ski trails, a sledding hill and abundant room for snowmobiling.

The modern shooting range is one of five available in the Michigan state park system, and it also offers a 25-position sporting clays course. Nature is not overlooked, and excellent hiking, birdwatching and wildflowers abound. The 4,637-acre park has something for everyone.

FEES: Daily $4, Annual $20, Senior Citizen Annual $5

DIRECTIONS: I-75 to exit 81. Go north on M-24 (Lapeer Road) approximately two miles to the park.

BEACH FINDER

PARK NAME	DELORME	UNIVERSAL
Bald Mountain Recreation Area	pg. 42, C1	map 63, H2

FURTHER INFORMATION: Bald Mountain Recreation Area, 1330 Greenshield Road, Route 1, Lake Orion, MI 48360 (248) 693-6767.

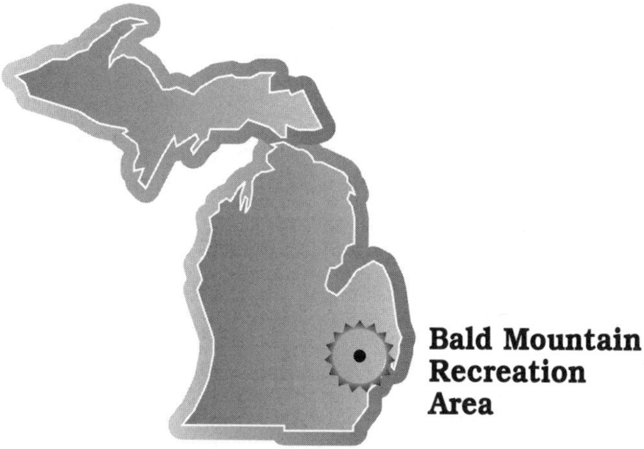

3 Belle Isle

In the center of the Detroit River between Detroit and Canada lies Belle Isle, a summer playground for Detroiters since the 1880s. In addition to its half-mile long beach, this unique island is home to a wealth of activities including the annual Detroit Grand Prix and the Thunderfest Hydroplane Boat Race.

Turn right after crossing the MacArthur Bridge and drive the perimeter of the 928-acre island for great views of the Detroit Renaissance Center, the Ambassador Bridge and Windsor. Enter the island's interior to see the huge Scott Memorial Fountain, built with the fortune of eccentric gambler James Scott. The Belle Island Aquarium, opened in 1904, is the oldest in America with 60 exhibits housing more than 1,300 specimens. The Anna Scripps Whitcomb Conservatory, patterned after Thomas Jefferson's Monticello, houses permanent displays of ferns, palms and cacti and has one of the largest orchid collections in the country. The Dossin Great Lakes Museum houses the world's largest collection of scale model Great Lakes ships and maritime memorabilia. The Belle Isle Zoo, open from May 1 through Oct. 31, was constructed in 1895. The renovated zoo now has a 3/4 -mile-long elevated boardwalk from which more than 25 species can be viewed. The island's nature center offers permanent displays as well as hosting special programs.

The bathing beach is located between the Detroit Yacht Club and MacArthur Bridge. The beach's most impressive feature is its waterslide, completed in 1996. The structure is actually three slides: an impressively high twisting slide for the adventurous, a mid-level slide and a gently inclined slide, all of which splash down into a common pool. Users must be 43 inches tall to ride.

Next to the slide is a bathhouse; snack concessions and additional picnic areas are found elsewhere on the island. A grassy strip leads to the half-mile-long by 50-foot-wide beach. The beach is surfaced with a coarse layer of gravel and sand, which changes to a band of clean sand at the shoreline. The river water is turbid but swimmable. The north facing view across the Detroit River is urban, with the downtown skyline and the bridge to the left. The beach opens up to a play and picnic area.

It's available for cooling off on a sticky day, but the beach is not the main reason to visit fascinating Belle Isle. The island is extremely popular and gets crowded during peak season, so it may be advisable to take advantage of Belle Isle's many wonders during cooler weather.

ABOUT THE PARK: Originally part of Ottawa and Chippewa territory, Belle Isle was called "White Swan" by native Americans. In the 1700s it was occupied by the French and the name was changed to Hog Island. The British then took over until Indians regained the territory and sold the swampy island to Lt. George McDougall in 1768 for eight barrels of rum, three rolls of tobacco and six pounds of red paint. The island changed hands several more times until it was sold to the city of Detroit in 1879.

In 1845 the name was changed to Belle Isle, reportedly to honor the governor's daughter, Miss Isabelle Cass. An architect was engaged in 1883 to prepare a plan to turn the island into a public park. Dredging operations created an interconnecting network of lakes and canals, and two manmade lakes were completed in the late 1800's. Land development and renovation continued over the decades, expanding the park from 690 acres to almost 1,000.

In addition to its main attractions the park offers bike paths, athletic fields, golf, tennis and racquetball courses, a driving range, fishing piers, a model yacht basin and 20 picnic shelters which are available for rental.

FEES: Nominal fees for some exhibits, $3 all day for the water-slide.

DIRECTIONS: From downtown Detroit, take Jefferson Avenue east to East Grand Boulevard. Cross the Douglas MacArthur Bridge at the Belle Isle sign. Follow the main road around the island. The beach is on Riverbank Road.

BEACH FINDER

PARK NAME	DELORME	UNIVERSAL
Belle Isle	pg. 34, B3	map 82, K7

FURTHER INFORMATION: City of Detroit, Belle Isle Administrative Office, Detroit MI 48207 (313) 852-4078

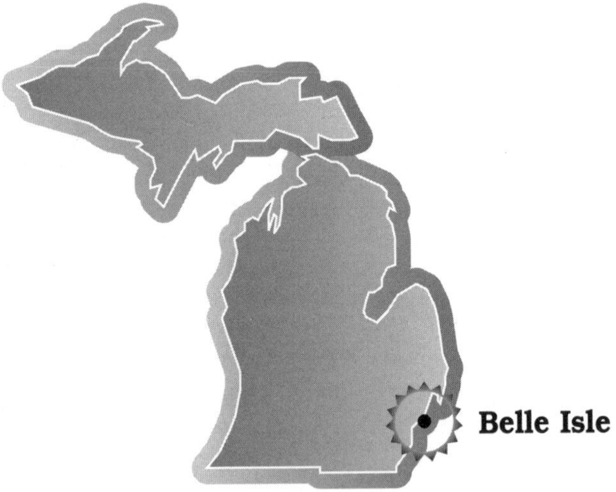

4 Brighton Recreation Area

Two lakes offer differing opportunities at this sprawling, almost 5,000 acre state park.

BISHOP LAKE

Brighton's original day use area is located at the northeast end of Bishop Lake. More a picnic area than a place to spread a blanket, the beach consists of only a small indentation in the lawn by the water's edge. The lawn, however, is huge and rolling and picnickers pull tables right up to the water to enjoy the view. Swimming is allowed all along the northeast face of the clear, soft-bottomed lake. A concession stand, volleyball court and playground are offered, as are boat rentals.

CHILSON POND

For those who enjoy a less domesticated beach with a wetlands, "up north" feel, or for anglers who want to find a beach where the kids can play while they fish, Chilson Pond fits the bill. This is Brighton's newest beach, where lilipads float just outside of the swimming area and fishermen in waders cast lines only yards from the swimmers.

A spacious lawn leads to a 500-foot-long by 50-foot-wide beach. The sand is coarse and gritty with a ragged, marshy shoreline.

The clear, brownish-tinted lake water has a soft, mucky floor. Canoes and small fishing boats drift by as the sounds of traffic mingle with the calls of wild birds. A concession stand, volleyball court, playground and boat rentals are offered, as well as four picnic shelters which are available for rental.

ABOUT THE PARK: Camping options are many at this popular park near Brighton. 150 modern sites are offered at Bishop Lake, while a total of 50 rustic sites are available at Appleton and Murray lakes. A special horseman-only campground of 25 rustic sites complements 18 miles of bridle trails in the park. Three frontier cabins and four family cabins may also be rented. The park's 10 lakes all offer fishing opportunities, with three boat-launch ramps available. Two hiking/biking trails, the two-mile Kahchin Trail and the five-mile Penosha Trail wind through field and forest. Winter pursuits include snowmobiling, cross-country skiing, ice fishing and skating. Hunting is allowed during legal seasons.

FEES: Daily $4, Annual $20, Senior Citizen Annual $5

DIRECTIONS: From I-96, take exit 147 (Spencer Road) and head west through the city of Brighton. Six miles outside of Brighton turn left (south) onto Chilson Road to Bishop Lake Road. Turn left (east) on Bishop Lake Road to the park entrance.

BEACH FINDER

PARK NAME	BEACH NAME	DELORME	UNIVERSAL
Brighton Recreation Area	Bishop Lake	pg. 32, A3 pg. 40, D3	map 47, C5
Brighton Recreation Area	Chilson Pond	pg. 40, D3	map 47, C4

FURTHER INFORMATION: Brighton Recreation Area, 6360 Chilson Road, Howell MI 48843 (810) 229-6566

Brighton
Recreation
Area

5 Dodge #4 State Park

Come early if you're planning to spend a summer's day at Cass Lake in Dodge #4 Park. The boat launch can fill up within the first two hours (the park opens at 8 a.m.) and you may find the closest parking lot to the beach to be full. This park, located in the heart of heavily populated Waterford Township, is popular primarily for its day-use facilities - boating, fishing, swimming and picnicking. The well-groomed flat lawn is nicely treed for shaded picnics. Grab a table behind the beach or cross the foot bridge to the large picnic area to the east. This area has no beach but the lake is easily accessible, and this is where boaters and Jet Skiers like to party. A separate bathhouse for this section is provided.

The Cass Lake beach is a small ribbon of sand, unfortunately shrunken due to high water levels and erosion. The 600 by 60-foot expanse barely holds the crowd, which, according to a ranger, is "standing room only" on weekends. The swimming area, however, compensates for the paucity of sand. The buoyed area is as long as the beach and, as the water remains shallow for a great distance, is enormously wide. Adults may feel like they are walking forever to get deep enough to take a plunge, but the shallowness provides a safe swim area for children. The width of the swim area allows the crowds and their profusion of tubes, rafts and floats to adequately spread out.

The sandy area has had its naturally smooth sand replaced with a coarser variety to fight erosion. The Huron River flows gently into Cass Lake, which is the largest of the chain of lakes in the

Waterford area. The water, although containing some light vegetative growth, is clean and clear to the bottom. In recent years zebra mussels have begun to appear, and a sign on the beach warns bathers that their shells can occasionally cut the feet of swimmers. The mussel problem is being monitored by the DNR and park personnel.

Cass Lake gets as deep as 100 feet and is excellent for fishing. It is stocked with trout and walleye, and a bass fishing tournament is held annually. In the winter, ice fishing is popular. Boats abound on Cass Lake. There is no "slow wake" zone in this part of the lake, so power boats and wave runners zoom noisily by. At the same time, sailboats, pontoons and sail-boarders provide quieter entertainment. Boats at anchor bob at both ends of the beach.

Full facilities are available, including a basic concession stand and an outside shower for rinsing. Boat rental is available at the concession stand, and two picnic shelters may also be rented. A paved path leads as far as the beach for wheelchair access.

ABOUT THE PARK: This busy state park is also southeast Michigan's smallest, at 139 acres. Cass Lake is noted for its fishing, especially around Gerundegut Bay at the west end of the lake. Largemouth and smallmouth bass, northern pike, panfish, lake trout and channel catfish are taken from the lake. A boat launch with space for 76 cars is near the bay. There are no campsites or hiking trails in the park.

FEES: Daily $4, Annual $20, Senior Citizen Annual $5

DIRECTIONS: From M-59 at Telegraph Road, take M-59 west 1 ½ miles to Cass Lake Road. Head south on Cass Lake Road to Cass-Elizabeth Lake Road. Head west on Cass-Elizabeth Lake Road, then turn left on Parkway Drive (opposite Mitch's Restaurant) to the park entrance.

BEACH FINDER

PARK NAME	DELORME	UNIVERSAL
Dodge #4 State Park	pg. 41, D7	map 63, G4

FURTHER INFORMATION: Dodge #4 State Park, 4250 Parkway Drive, Waterford MI 48328 (248) 666-1020

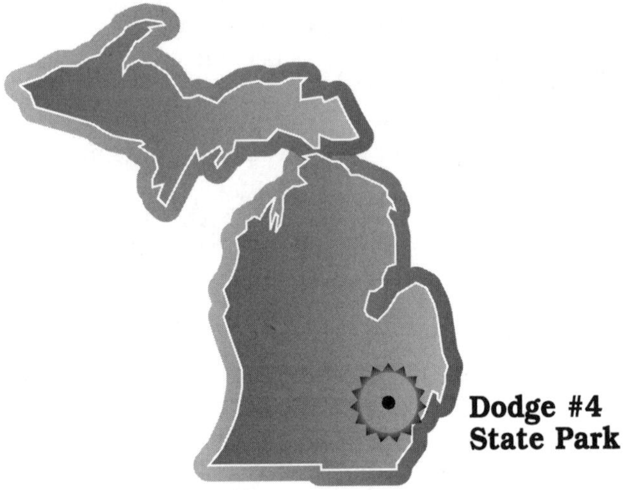

6 Groveland Oaks County Park

Bustling is the word for this spirited Oakland County park. A large lawn with picnic tables and grills leads to Stewart Lake, where kids flock to a huge, twisting water slide. Fees are 50 cents a ride or $5 for the entire day.

Camping opportunities include modern, semi-modern and primitive sites, so everything from huge trailers to tents can be accommodated. Unfortunately there is no campers' beach, so day users and overnight guests all crowd onto the 400- by 50-foot beach and spill onto the lawn. Swimming includes two roped and guarded areas with a floating dock in the deep end. The lake is clean with a soft sand bottom, but the restricted swimming tends to jam bathers together.

Paddleboats can be rented by crossing a picturesque bridge to the rental building. There's also a half-court for basketball, horseshoe pits, volleyball, a softball field and a large pavilion. The attractive concession building has a terrace facing the lake. The children's playscape is like a real-life Chutes and Ladders game with interconnected bridges, towers and slides, and spacious wooden benches for attentive parents. There's even a wading pool near group campgrounds at the north end of the park.

Not a beach for communing with nature, but one where the kids sure won't get bored.

FEES: $5 for Oakland county residents, $8 for non-residents

DIRECTIONS: I-75 to exit 101 (Grange Hall Road). East on Grange Hall Road to Dixie Highway. Left on Dixie, park entrance is ¼ mile on the right.

BEACH FINDER

PARK NAME	DELORME	UNIVERSAL
Groveland Oaks County Park	pg. 41, B5	map 63, F1

FURTHER INFORMATION: Groveland Oaks County Park, 14555 Dixie Highway, Holly MI (248) 634-9811

Groveland Oaks County Park

7 HOLLY RECREATION AREA

Whether you're seeking the solitude of a northern Michigan lake or enjoying the bustle of crowds and people-watching, the two beaches at the Holly Recreation Area will suit your needs.

HERON LAKE

The day use area at Heron Lake offers one of the largest beaches in Oakland County. At about an eighth of a mile by 100 feet wide, the beach is large enough to accommodate a volleyball court at the north end, a slide near the south end, and swings in the middle. The south/southwest lake frontage keeps bathers facing the sun all day.

The fine sand is mixed with pebbles. The swimming is delightful - the buoyed swim area is as long as the beach and the clear brownish-green lake water is fresh and mostly free of plant debris. Heron Lake also holds a natural wonder: cool artesian spring water wells up from the earth, producing a 20 foot damp border of sand along the water's edge. Rivulets of fresh water which seem to come from nowhere trickle down the beach and run into the lake. The wettest area tops a manmade drainage field hidden under the sand. This natural spring area is so abundant that without the addition of drain tiles, this area of the beach would wash away.

Bring a diving mask and you can hunt for a pipe that is buried under the beach and ends underwater in the swimming area, spilling out clear spring water. Take a walk toward the west end of the beach along the water's edge and look for the tiny swirling pool of water and sand in front of the swing set. That's a natural spring, an icy cold whirlpool bubbling up amid the warm lake water.

Gasoline motors are not allowed on Heron Lake, but fishermen are allowed to troll quietly for largemouth bass and panfish. A boat launch and picnic area are located around the west side of the lake from the beach and feature a wooden fishing dock, tables, grills and an outhouse.

Beach goers can cruise around this fairly large lake in canoes, paddleboats or rowboats available for rental at the concession stand. Picnickers will find a sprawling lawn strewn with tables and grills. Full facilities are available including a concession stand (the Road Kill Grill) with the standard fare, a convenient spigot for rinsing feet when leaving the beach and handicapped access up to the beach area.

WILDWOOD LAKE

Even on a hot sunny Sunday in June, the beach at Wildwood Lake was practically deserted, the perfect getaway for those seeking the peacefulness of chirping birds and still water. This beach is definitely rustic in comparison to the beach on Heron Lake. In addition to the buoyed swimming area there are a bathhouse, picnic tables and barbecues, but even with these amenities this area retains a surprisingly remote feeling. A warning to people with boom-boxes... park rangers will shoot first and ask questions later.

There's a gently rolling hill/meadow bordered and dotted with huge shade trees that provide relief from the scalding sun even on the hottest of summer days. The water is cool and refreshing and has the typical brown-green tint of a small inland lake. Beyond the buoyed swimming area you can see the tips of water plants breaking the surface of the lake, giving it a wilder than average appearance.

It's a long and scenic drive getting to Wildwood Lake, just east of Heron Lake and connected to the smaller Valley Lake. A rolling hill with a manicured lawn and picnic area lead down to the small 100-foot by 300-foot beach. Like Heron Lake, Wildwood Lake originally was a wetlands area, and a manmade dam controls the flow of water from nearby Thread Creek. A boat launch leads to excellent bass fishing in Wildwood Lake.

ABOUT THE PARK: There are actually 17 lakes of varying sizes within the Holly Recreation Area. Birdwatching is a popular occupation, as are fishing, hiking, and camping. A campground at McGinnis Lake offers both improved and rustic sites, and there is also an organizational campground available for group usage. A six-bunk frontier cabin may also be rented.

Take a short hike on the eighth-of-a-mile Blue Trail, investigate the 5.6-mile Red Trail, or plan to tackle all 23 miles of foot trails. Although there are no riding stables in the park, seven miles of bridle trails and an equestrian staging area are available to horseback riders. The winter finds cross-country ski trails and snowmobile trails provided, and much of the park is open to hunters.

FEES: Daily $4, Annual $20, Senior Citizen Annual $5

DIRECTIONS: From I-75, take exit 101 (Grange Hall Road). Follow Grange Hall Road east. When the road forks, bear right onto McGinnis Road. The entrance to the day use area is on the right.

FURTHER INFORMATION: Holly Recreation Area, 8100 Grange Hall Road, Holly, MI 48442 (248) 634-8811

BEACH FINDER

PARK NAME	BEACH NAME	DELORME	UNIVERSAL
Holly Recreation Area	Heron Lake	pg. 41, B5	map 63, F1
Brighton Recreation Area	Wildwood Lake	pg. 41, B5	map 63, F1

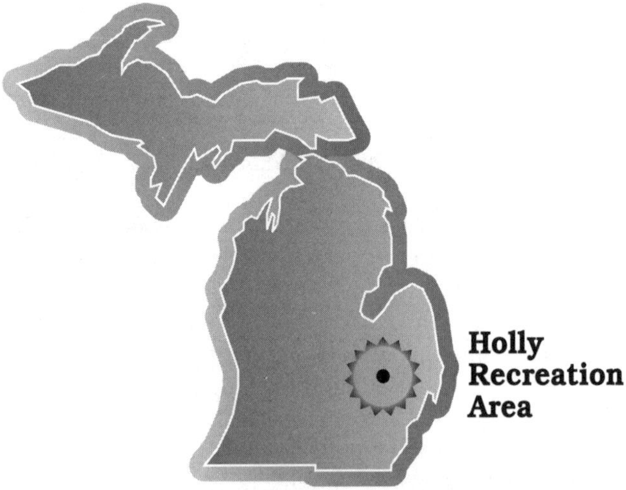

8 Independence Lake County Park

This Washtenaw County Park north of Ann Arbor is noted for its uniquely varied habitat. Incorporating a tall-grass prairie, swampy marsh, old meadows, mature hardwoods and a beach, Independence Lake Park is home to many species, including several on the threatened and endangered lists.

A massive lawn rolls gently to the lake from a gravel parking lot. There's a smattering of picnic tables under a cool stand of oaks, but bring blankets or chairs for sunning. To the left of the main area is another huge picnic lawn with a terrific wooden playscape for kids, volleyball courts and a horseshoe pit. A handicapped accessible fishing pier juts into the lake at its north side.

Two small sandy beaches indent the meadow on either side of a roped and buoyed but generously sized swim area. Two lifeguards protect swimmers. There is another swimming area and guard tower and three more small sandy inlets that can handle overflow crowds, but if a lifeguard is not on duty then swimming is not allowed. However, the moderate crowd on the July weekend we visited was manageable. The sand is coarse but not stony; the lake water is brownish and alive with darting minnows. Rowboats and canoes can be rented by the hour, and a boat launch is located at the southwest side of the lake. Bring your own goodies, as there's no food concession at the park.

ABOUT THE PARK: Independence Lake County Park is perfect for group usage. Four pavilions are available on a rental basis. Beach Center, Independence Woods, Meadow's Edge, and The Group Center offer many amenities, with the latter seating up to 480 adults. All have group size barbecue grills. A mile long nature trail winds through the park. The park is open daily from Memorial Day through Labor Day, and weekends only in May and September.

FEES: $3 Washtenaw county resident, $6 non-resident

DIRECTIONS: From U.S. 23, exit at Six Mile Road. Follow signs about four miles to the park entrance.

BEACH FINDER

PARK NAME	DELORME	UNIVERSAL
Independence Lake County Park	pg. 32, A3	map 81, C6

FURTHER INFORMATION: Independence Lake County Park, 3200 Jennings Road, Whitmore Lake MI (734) 449-4437

Independence Lake County Park

9 Independence Oaks County Park

Part of the 11 park Oakland County system, Independence Oaks is one of the more unique, if small, parks in the metropolitan Detroit area.

The park's large body of naturally spring-fed water, Crooked Lake, had an underwater drop-off too steep for a safe swimming beach. So in 1976 a manmade lake (more appropriately described as a large pond), Hidden Springs, was created from wetlands southeast of the big lake. Even with a blanket of coarse sand the lake floor was soft and muddy. In 1986 the county improved the lake by excavating the sand, installing a clay lining and then replacing the sand.

In 1992 the lake was again improved, as a pipeline was run 15 feet uphill from Crooked Lake. Fresh lakewater now is pumped in from Crooked Lake to the north side of Hidden Springs, and flows out through a weir on the south side into the Clinton River, the headwaters of which pass through the park. Three aerators made of fiberglass cleverly disguised as rocks circulate the water. This constant flow makes Hidden Springs more like a river than a lake. The water is clean, clear, remarkably free of plant debris, and produces extremely low levels of bacteria. The influx of fresh water from Crooked Lake keeps Hidden Springs comfortably cool even in the heat of summer.

The bathing area is only four feet deep, but if you are a good swimmer the lifeguards will permit you to swim to a floating dock where you can practice diving into 12 feet of water. On the down side, with three lifeguard stands and a grid of ropes and buoys, it can feel like swimming in the natural equivalent of an Olympic pool.

The beach fronting this small lake is smaller still. A mere 30-foot by 90-yard strip of course sand separates the manicured lawn and picnic area from the lake. The up-to-date children's playground is abundant with equipment, modern bathroom facilities and a concession stand that sells everything from food to rafts make this a desirable haven for young families. Even though we consider this beach to be a hidden jewel, it's diminutive size makes it more like a half-carat zircon than a five-carat diamond.

ABOUT THE PARK: Independence Oaks is a lovely park, well worth visiting for its hiking trails, boating facilities and outstanding nature center which doubled in size in 1996. Its nearly 1,100 acres are rated as one of the highest quality wetland habitants in Oakland County by the Michigan Natural Features Inventory. Its eight hiking trails include one which is paved for handicapped accessibility, and all are groomed in winter for cross-country skiing.

Pedal boats, rowboats, and canoes are available for rental, as are skis during the winter months. Numerous picnic pavilions may also be rented. Docks and a boat ramp provide easy access to Crooked Lake, and a 200-seat amphitheater hosts special musical, theatrical, and nature programs throughout the summer.

FEES: $5 for Oakland County residents, $8 for non-residents, $2 for senior citizens (weekdays only). $25 annual resident fee, $45 non-resident, $15 senior citizen

DIRECTIONS: I-75 north from Pontiac to exit 89 (Sashabaw Road). North on Sashabaw for two miles, past Clarkston Road and Pine Knob, to the park entrance.

BEACH FINDER

PARK NAME	DELORME	UNIVERSAL
Independence Oaks County Park	pg. 41, B6	map 63, G2

FURTHER INFORMATION: Independence Oaks County Park, 9501 Sashabaw Rd., Clarkston, MI 48348. (248) 625-0877 Nature Center (248) 625-6473

10 Island Lake Recreation Area

Beach Freaks will find two very different beaching experiences at Kent Lake and Spring Mill Pond, the two swimming areas at Island Lake Recreation Area, a 4,000 acre state park in Livingston County. A third beach, at Island Lake, was closed when wave runners and motor boats originating from the privately owned side of the lake got unmanageable and made swimming hazardous.

KENT LAKE

The huge, treed, manicured lawn leading to Kent Lake at the eastern end of Island Lake Recreation Area makes for an attractive view. This arm of Kent Lake, the majority of which runs through Kensington Metropark, is shallow, warm and nicely swimmable. The beach itself is a narrow, ¼-mile curve which is sprawling enough to handle a crowd. The coarse sand is pebbly and rough on the feet, and dirt in the sand prompts vegetation to sprout. The poor sand quality is unfortunate, because the Kent Lake site is otherwise appealing.

Canoeing is popular in the park, as the Huron River winds its way across Island's Lake's center. Heavner Canoe Rental has a concession right on the Kent Lake beach, and canoes may be rented for trips from two hours to an entire day. Trips to the River Bend and Placeway picnic areas or to U.S. 23 can be arranged, with Heavner picking up paddlers at a pre-arranged time. Paddleboats and rowboats are also available for rental.

A small fishing dock juts into Kent Lake next to the beach, where fishermen will find bluegills, perch and bass. Boats drift peacefully by, but a small distraction comes from the steady hum of traffic and glimpses through the trees of the I-96 freeway. The beach is not easily accessible to wheelchairs, as there is no paved path, and the wooden curbing from the lawn to the beach is steep in places.

SPRING MILL POND

Spring Mill Pond left these Beach Freaks depressed. Scrubby pines and immature maples on a weedy meadow lead to a small pond and a beach strewn with bird droppings. The water is rusty brown; the sand pebbly and coarse. A concrete sidewalk running from the parking lot to the beach makes it handicapped accessible, although one must again beware of those goose poop landmines. A tiny concession stand sells microwaved sandwiches and snacks, and also rents oversized rafts and a paddleboat. There are grills and tables, although we found it an unappealing site for a picnic. The best feature of the park is the restrooms, which are new and numerous. Spring Mill Pond is the site of a special catch-and-release early trout season during April. Best leave this beach to the fishes.

ABOUT THE PARK: The Island Lake Recreation Area offers facilities for two activities never dreamed of when the park was set up by the auto manufacturing Dodge brothers in 1927 - hot air ballooning and mountain biking. The only balloonport in a Michigan state park is located at the Meadow Picnic Area, and balloons may be viewed taking off during the May to September flying season. Mountain bikes are welcome on the 14 mile trail that loops around the Huron River, passing through picturesque marshes, woods and fields. Bikers share the woodland trail with runners, hikers, and even hunters in season.

The park also has a campground offering 20 modern sites at East Beach, 25 rustic sites at Russell Woods, and a small canoe campground accessible only from the river. Two frontier cabins with bunks for 20, and a youth organizational campground may be reserved in advance.

The park is open all winter, permitting snowmobiling, cross-country skiing, and hunting. Five picnic sites with shelters and outhouse facilities may be rented for special events.

FEES: Daily $4, Annual $20, Senior Citizen Annual $5

DIRECTIONS: From I-96, take exit 151 (Kensington Road). Park exit is 3/4 of a mile south.

BEACH FINDER

PARK NAME	BEACH NAME	DELORME	UNIVERSAL
Island Lake Recreation Area	Kent Lake	pg. 41, D4	map 63, E4 map 47, D5
Island Lake Recreation Area	Spring Mill Pond	pg. 41, D4	map 63, E4 map 47, D5

FURTHER INFORMATION: Island Lake Recreation Area, 12950 E. Grand River Ave., Brighton MI 48116. (810) 229-7067

Island Lake
Recreation
Area

11 Kensington Metropark

The big daddy of all the metroparks is Kensington, a 4,337-acre facility surrounding Kent Lake. Offering everything from a farm center to a golf course, swimming at one of Kensington's two beaches is only one of many activities for a family to enjoy.

MAPLE BEACH

Located on the west side of huge Kent Lake is popular Maple Beach. The enormous parking lot is an indicator of the numbers that gather on summer weekends, but the beach is spacious enough to handle the crowd. A manicured lawn slopes to the large concession building and beach. There are no picnic tables or grills by the beach, but you'll find 12 picnic areas scattered around Kent Lake.

The large beach is well maintained and monitored. Swimming is controlled, with two or three roped sections open as needed and six lifeguards monitoring the activity. Floats are permitted in the children's swimming section only. The sand is dark, coarse and stiff but is free of pebbles and stones. A boat rental building is near Maple Beach, and sailboats, paddleboats and rowboats as well as bicycles may be rented. Snacks are sold at the boat rental building as well as at the beachhouse.

A volleyball court is located at the east side of the beach, and concrete animals make up a play area for the little ones. A paved path to the beach allows wheelchair accessibility. Maple Beach is the site of a Detroit Symphony Orchestra concert and fireworks on the Fourth of July.

MARTINDALE BEACH

Across Kent Lake from Maple Beach is its twin, Martindale Beach. Similar in size, with the same sand quality and arrangement, Martindale also attracts large summer crowds. A hike/bike trail runs through Martindale, which also features a ball field and a modern playscape for kids.

The roped swimming area has two to five areas open as needed, with up to eight lifeguards monitoring the action. There is also a large bathhouse with a food concession, and a paved path and ramp which leads to the lake.

ABOUT THE PARK: This unit of the Huron-Metropolitan Authority is an all-sports facility. Boaters can launch at two ramps and rent slips at three docking areas. The Island Queen, a 66-passenger Sternwheeler makes hourly trips for individuals and groups. An 18-hole par 71 public golf course is located at the south end of Kent Lake and a Farm Center offers the sights and sounds of old-fashioned farm life. A Nature Center and Study Area is the entryway to four labeled trails ranging from ½ mile to 2½ miles in length. The nature center offers nature walks and special activities throughout the year.

Eight miles of hiking and biking trails offer clear sailing for roller bladers and joggers. A 20-station exercise trail is located at the Playfield Picnic Area, and 10 miles of equestrian trails are available for those with their own mounts. In winter the golf starter building becomes a Ski Touring Center, with ski rentals available. Tobogganing and sledding take place at the Orchard Picnic Area and ice skating, lighted on the weekends, starts at the boat rental building. Year-round group camp sites can be reserved for overnight and day camping.

FEES: $2 weekdays, $3 weekends and holidays, $15 annual

DIRECTIONS: From I-96, exit at either Kensington Road or Kent Lake Road. Head north from either exit to the park entrance.

BEACH FINDER

PARK NAME	BEACH NAME	DELORME	UNIVERSAL
Kensington Metropark	Maple Beach	pg. 41, D4	map 63, E4 map 47, D5
Kensington Metropark	Martindale Beach	pg. 41, D4	map 63, E4 map 47, D5

FURTHER INFORMATION: Kensington Metropark, 2240 W. Bruno Road, Milford MI 48380 (248) 685-1561 or 1-800-477-3178

12 Metamora-Hadley Recreation Area

The day use area at the Metamora-Hadley Recreation Area is small but pleasant. The beach is larger than at first view and the wide lawn affords plenty of picnicking room. The beach is on a small arm at the north end of Lake Minnawanna. The view from most of the beach is of the park campground only a hundred yards across the water, and the sight of tents and trailers is hardly scenic. But spread your blanket at the east end of the beach and you look out at the length of the 80-acre lake and its densely wooded surroundings.

The beach is 350 feet long by 100 feet wide. The sand is tan and fine, sprinkled lightly with pebbles. The buoyed swimming area extends the length of the beach but is narrow, not extending out very far into the water. Lake Minnawanna is fed from Fisherman's Creek, and the water is clean and clear. A harvesting program keeps weeds in the swimming area under control. As the rest of the lake is shallow and weedy, it does not attract an abundance of power boats. The day of our visit found only rowboats, canoes, and trolling fishing boats. Rowboats, canoes, and paddleboats may be rented at the beach concession stand, as can "floating islands" for $4 an hour. A small fishing pier is located at the west end of the beach.

A concession stand and separate men's and women's bathhouses with indoor showers are provided. For those feeling energetic, off of the beach parking lot is the entrance to more than six miles of marked hiking trails.

ABOUT THE PARK: Lake Minnawanna sits at the center of this 723 acre park, which provides a boat launch and three fishing piers for anglers. More than two-thirds of the park is open for hunting both large and small game. 224 modern, shaded campsites are available, with several sites offering spectacular views of the lake. Two mini-cabins which sleep four and one picnic shelter may be rented. In winter semi-modern camping, ice-fishing, cross-country skiing and snowmobiling are available.

FEES: Daily $4, Annual $20, Senior Citizen Annual $5

DIRECTIONS: From M-24 (Lapeer Road) turn west onto Pratt Road, then two miles to Hurd Road. Turn left (south) on Hurd Road to the park entrance.

BEACH FINDER

PARK NAME	DELORME	UNIVERSAL
Metamora-Hadley Recreation Area	pg. 41, A7	map 44, C14

FURTHER INFORMATION: Metamora-Hadley Recreation Area, 3871 Hurd Road, Metamora, MI 48455 (810) 797-4439

Metamora-Hadley Recreation Area

The waterslide at Metro Beach Metropark.

13 Metro Beach Metropark

The Metro Beach Metropark can best be described as an entertainment complex that includes a wonderful beach on Lake St. Clair. For those not interested in the beach there's the alternative of an Olympic size swimming pool with a diving board and 120-foot-long water slide, an 18 hole miniature golf course, a twenty-station exercise trail, four tennis courts, 20 shuffleboard courts and three marinas with transient accommodations for 320 boats.

Beach lovers will be impressed by the 3,000-foot beach that looks out over Lake St. Clair's vast horizon. It's a "big water" feel, with boats mere dots in the distance and choppy surf that's fun to frolic in. The beach is made up of that unfortunate mixture of coarse brown sand and pebbles, but at least there's an abundance of it. The swimming area is guarded, with seven guard stands used as needed. The swim area is buoyed but not roped, and the 10 foot depth allows for plenty of room to spread out. Unlike calm inland lakes the water is always moving, crashing musically against the shoreline. The August day we visited found the water clean, clear and refreshing.

Mention must be made of the periods of unacceptably high bacteria levels in the water, which occasionally cause the beach to close. The situation has improved since its peak in 1993, and the water quality is tested every two days.

Picnicking is confined to designated areas in the park, so the sprawling lawn that borders the beach has no tables or grills. Facilities are first-rate, from the large, efficient concession building with its spacious patio to the separate beach store. The concrete sidewalk leading to the various outbuildings is called the "boardwalk," and there actually is a short stretch of real boardwalk to stroll upon or sit on benches and watch the crowd. The Tot Lot and Play Lot for children ages 2 through 10 is impressive with colorful, modern climbing equipment, a unique maze and even little kid-sized houses. Comfortable rocking wooden gliders ring the area for waiting parents.

ABOUT THE PARK: Besides the facilities mentioned above, nature is not forgotten in the 770-acre park. There's a nature center and labeled nature trails which extend into adjacent

woods, meadows and marshes. Boaters may use the eight available boat ramps or the launching area for sailboats and sailboards. In winter, cross-country ski equipment can be rented for use on the 2.5 miles of trails. Rinks for ice skating and ice hockey are provided and ice fishing is permitted at the North Marina.

Private groups can reserve one of the many shelters or picnic canopies in the park, and there's even a tram to shuttle visitors from the main parking lot to picnic sites on Huron Point.

FEES: \$3 weekends, \$2 weekdays, \$15 annual, \$8 senior citizen annual

DIRECTIONS: From Detroit, take I-94 east to exit 236 (Metropolitan Parkway). Turn right off of the exit and go approximately three miles to the park entrance.

BEACH FINDER

PARK NAME	DELORME	UNIVERSAL
Metro Beach Metropark	pg. 43, D4	map 50, M4

FURTHER INFORMATION: Metro Beach Metropark, 31300 Metro Parkway, P.O. Box 46905, Mt. Clemens, MI 48046 (810) 463-4581

Metro Beach
Metropark

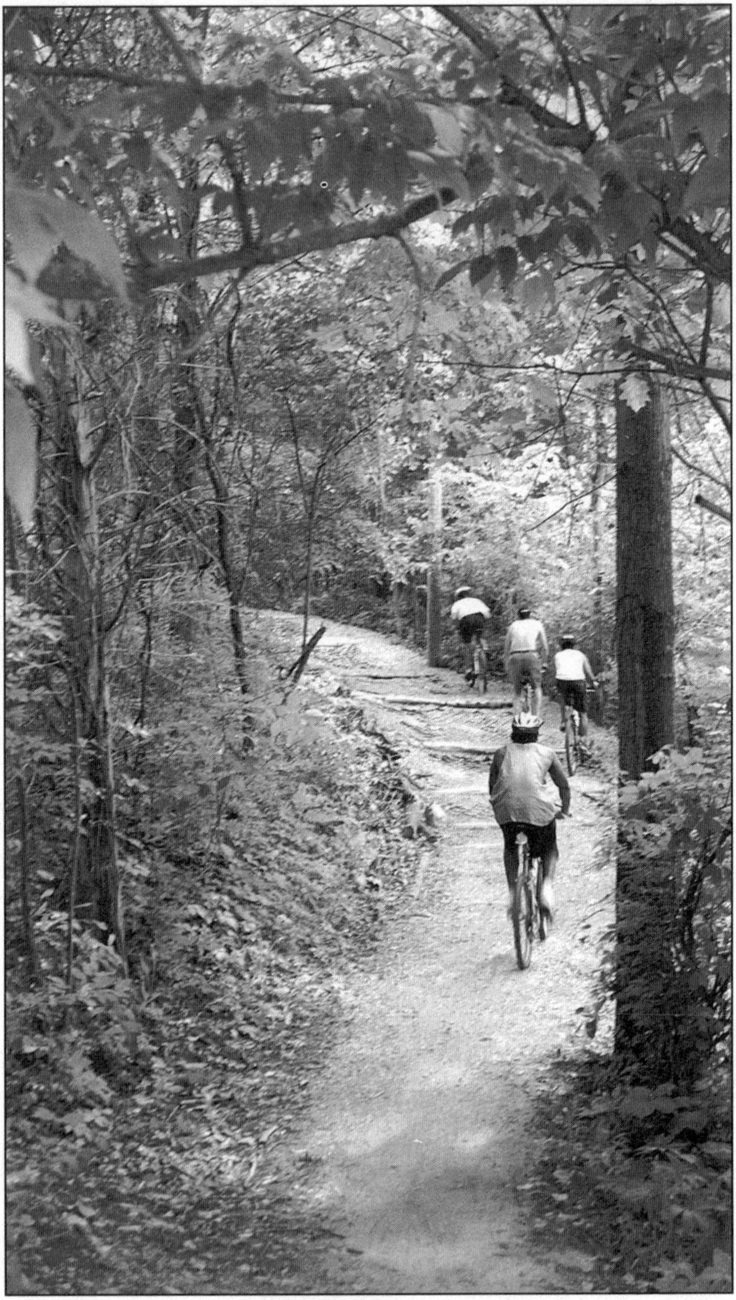

14 Pickney Recreation Area

With 10 lakes to its credit, the Pickney Recreation Area offers only two swimming areas, Silver Lake and Half Moon Beach. But this popular park has much to recommend a visit.

HALF MOON BEACH

The Half Moon Lake day use area isn't quite the place that it used to be. In 1994 a tornado carried away the roof of the restroom/concession building and ripped through a stand of mature oak trees. Today the site has only porta-johns and no concessions, so bring your own snacks if you plan to spend the day.

Half Moon Lake is part of a chain of seven lakes connected by streams and channels, all of which are navigable by canoe or boat. Only the eastern arm of the 236-acre lake is visible from the day use area, giving the impression that the lake is much smaller than it is. On the eastern tip of the lake lies Half Moon Beach, a pleasantly sprawling clover-strewn lawn with a small 200-foot beach.

Surrounded by private homes, Half Moon feels more like a private lake that a state park. Motor boats and Jet Skis abound, whizzing noisily close to the swimming area. The buoyed swim area extends along the entire eastern end of the lake, but doesn't extend very far from the shore as the lake deepens quickly. Half Moon Lake offers a public boat launch, and boaters often anchor on the northeast side of the lake to go picnicking on the grounds.

DIRECTIONS: From U.S. 23, take exit 49 (North Territorial Road). Head west on North Territorial for 12 miles, then turn right on Hankerd Road. The road winds to the entrance of Half Moon Beach.

BEACH FINDER

PARK NAME	BEACH NAME	DELORME	UNIVERSAL
Pickney Recreation Area	Half Moon Beach	pg. 32, A2	map 81, B6

SILVER LAKE

The most instantly noticeable feature of Silver Lake Beach is that there's no beach at all, not even a sandy drop-off into the lake. But that didn't seem to bother the enthusiastic crowd who spread blankets on the neatly manicured lawn and frolicked in the clear, spring-fed water of Silver Lake. Even without a beach, there's a lot to recommend the Silver Lake site.

You can't miss the numerous bike racks atop the cars filling the large parking lot. Silver Lake is the starting point for the park's hiking and mountain biking trails, including the 17 mile long Potawatomi Trail, which winds its way through the entire park. Hikers and bikers start at different access points and travel in opposite directions. A new hikers only trail, the Losee Lake Hiking Trail, travels a gentle 1.5 to 3.3 miles and is also accessed off of the Silver Lake parking lot.

Five sand volleyball courts line the lawn, and the park sponsors tournaments with cash prizes throughout the summer. Turn right to a play area with slides, swings and a merry-go-round. Pass the playground and an attractive wooden fishing dock juts into lilipad strewn water. Next to the dock are rowboats, canoes and Jurassic-vintage paddleboats, which may be rented at the concession stand.

The sprawling lawn comes right up to the water and in some places sits too high above the lake for access. When we visited

Silver Lake, high water levels caused severe erosion and we could see exposed soil under the lawn eroding into the lake. But there were still many spots to ease into the sandy-bottomed lake. The spring-fed water is clean, clear, and free of plant debris. The buoyed, five-foot-deep swim area covers the entire frontage of the 204-acre lake. A small peninsula juts into the southeast end of the lake, and this is a picturesque spot for a picnic. Although it is not a buoyed swim area, the rangers seemed to have no problem with folks swimming around the peninsula.

There is no boat launch at Silver Lake, so the only motor boats are those belonging to residents of the private homes on the northeast side of the lake. On the windy day that we visited, wind-surfers colorfully dotted the waters. A large sandbox on the lawn gives kids a place to dig, and full concession and restroom facilities complete the picture. Silver Lake is one of the nicest beachless beaches around.

ABOUT THE PARK: Pickney is one of the largest, at more than 10,000 acres, and most popular of southeast Michigan's state parks. One of its outstanding features is its lakes, which offer numerous opportunities for fishing and canoeing. There are 10 lakes in all, seven of which are connected by channels. Except for Silver Lake, which allows car-top and rental boats only, all of the lakes have boat launch facilities. Bass, panfish, pike and bluegill are the primary catches for anglers.

Hiking, backpacking and mountain biking are also primary features of the park. Forty miles of trails wind through the park, from gentle trails of just over a mile to the northern half of the Waterloo-Pickney Trail, a 42-mile, three-day hike. The Lakelands Trail, still under construction, can be picked up at the D-19 carpool lot in Pickney. This trail will eventually continue for 31 miles, from Jackson to Hamburg.

A modern campground at Bruin Lake features 220 partially wooded sites. Two smaller rustic campgrounds are also available. There is an equestrian staging area off of Monk Road, and five miles of available bridle trails. A private stable, Hell Creek Ranch, is located outside of the park on Cedar Lake Road and uses the park's bridle trails. Winter finds ice fishing, snowmobiling and cross-country skiing on some of the park's hiking trails. Hunting is available in part of the park, primarily for rabbits and deer.

FEES: Daily $4, Annual $20, Senior Citizen Annual $5

DIRECTIONS: From U.S. 23, take exit 49 to North Territorial Road. Turn right (north) on Dexter-Townhall Road to the park entrance.

BEACH FINDER

PARK NAME	BEACH NAME	DELORME	UNIVERSAL
Pickney Recreation Area	Silver Lake	pg. 32, A2	map 81, B6

FURTHER INFORMATION: Pickney Recreation Area, 8555 Silver Hill, Route 1, Pickney, MI 48169 (734) 426-4913

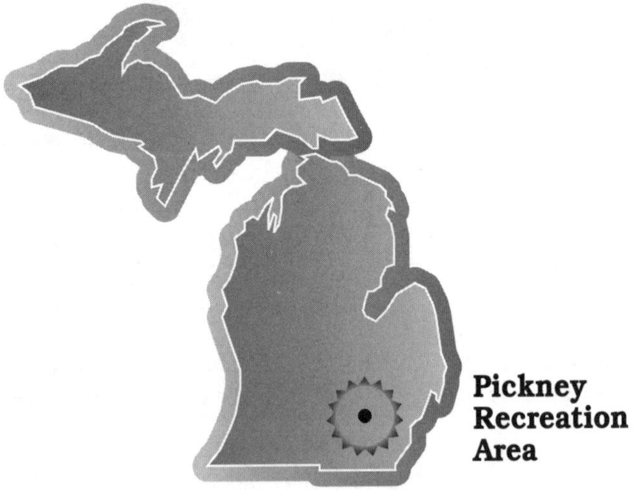

15 Pontiac Lake Recreation Area

For a real "day at the beach" try the ⅓ of a mile long stretch of sand fronting Pontiac Lake in Waterford Township. The beach is surprisingly spacious (it's 160 feet wide) with brownish-tan sand that is much finer and softer than at many metropolitan area beaches. This is sand worth burrowing your toes in! Pontiac Lake can attract as many as 3,000 cars on a busy weekend, but its size easily disperses the crowd. Quiet it's not - power boats and Jet Skis zoom by and small planes from the nearby Pontiac/Oakland airport buzz overhead.

The swim area extends the entire third of a mile, but as the lake drops off quickly the buoyed area does not extend very far into the water. This large lake was created by damming the Huron River, and it hosts an unusual feature - tiny Gale Island perched in the middle of the lake. A sprinkling of small houses are clearly visible from the beach, and at this writing two families reside there year-round. They commute to the island by boat before the freeze, by pickup truck over the ice after the freeze, and by pushing a small boat onto the ice at the thaw.

The problem of weeds which long haunted Pontiac Lake is now well managed with chemical treatment and mechanical harvesting. Watch out for a line of swan droppings amid the vegetation at the shoreline. Although the beach is frequently groomed the park rangers can't quite keep up with the pesky swans. The beach area also features a large, flat lawn for picnics and three shelters and two canopies which can be rented. These areas are all near bathhouses or have access to outhouses. Volleyball nets can be found at either side of the beach and also at the picnic shelters. Children's play equipment is located on both sides of a traditional concession stand. Also available for day use are a baseball diamond and a half basketball court.

ABOUT THE PARK: The 3,800-acre park features three campgrounds, the largest of which is a modern facility with 176 sites. There is also an equestrian staging area and campground and an organizational campground, both of which are rustic with few facilities. The Pontiac Lake Riding Stable offers horseback riding along the park's 17 miles of trails as well as pony rides, riding lessons, group rides and hayrides. There is also a popular 11 mile mountain biking trail and a 1.9-mile hiking trail.

A boat launch at the east end of the lake leads to excellent bass fishing. Hunting is allowed in season, and the park is open for snowmobiling and cross-country skiing, although trails are not specified for these activities. A supervised rifle range, a shotgun range, and an archery range are also located within the park.

FEES: Daily $4, Annual $20, Senior Citizen Annual $5

DIRECTIONS: From M-59, drive north on Williams Lake Road. Turn left at Gale Road and follow the signs to the park.

BEACH FINDER

PARK NAME	DELORME	UNIVERSAL
Pontiac Lake Recreation Area	pg. 41, C6	map 63, F3

FURTHER INFORMATION: Pontiac Lake Recreation Area, 7800 Gale Road, Waterford MI 48327 (248) 666-1020

Pontiac Lake Recreation Area

16 Proud Lake Recreation Area

"The old swimming hole" is the phrase that comes to mind at Powers Beach, the day use facility at the Proud Lake Recreation Area. A tiny 18-by 100-foot beach fronts a pond that is an offshoot of the Huron River, which is fed by Proud Lake to the east.

The buoyed swimming area is small and rapidly gets crowded. The trucked-in sand is soft and damp, a result of springs feeding the pond. The lawn/picnic area behind the beach is limited but extends off of the parking lot to the west and is hilly, heavily treed and offers grills and tables. There is a rental picnic shelter close to the pond and a second shelter near the park entrance. Play equipment, a volleyball net and a ball field are available in the picnic area.

Across the pond from the beach is a small island connected by two foot bridges. Bathers can walk out on the island or fish from it. Canoers paddling down the Huron River drift in and out of the pond or pull up along the shore to picnic. Canoes can be rented in the park south of Powers Beach or at the campground. Facilities are limited to restrooms and changing rooms, which unfortunately have no doors. There is also no handicapped accessible path from the parking lot.

Campers and boaters have a separate beach on Proud Lake, so this small swimming hole is basically a place for picnickers to cool off, and is not recommended for families looking to spend a day sunning and swimming.

ABOUT THE PARK: The 4,000-acre park boasts a modern campground with 130 sites and two mini-cabins, as well as two rustic organizational camps. An outdoor center complex is comprised of three dormitories, an activities building and a modern kitchen/dining hall (call 248-685-2433 for reservations). A horseman's staging area is located in the middle of an extensive network of dual use bridle and mountain biking trails. Hiking and ski trails run through forests, fields, and wetlands. For fishermen, a two-mile stretch of the Huron River is stocked with trout each spring, and the park's two lakes, Proud Lake and Moss Lake, are abundant with bass, pike, sunfish and crappies. Hunting is permitted in parts of the park and boaters can access Proud Lake at the Bass Lake Road boat launch.

FEES: Daily $4, Annual $20, Senior Citizen Annual $5

DIRECTIONS: From Detroit, take I-96 to exit 159 (Wixom Road). Follow Wixom Road north and watch the park signs for the Powers Beach entrance.

BEACH FINDER

PARK NAME	BEACH NAME	DELORME	UNIVERSAL
Proud Lake Recreation Area	Powers Beach	pg. 41, D5	map 63, F4

FURTHER INFORMATION: Proud Lake Recreation Area, 3500 Wixom Road, Milford MI 48382 (248) 685-2433

17 Seven Lakes State Park

There are six lakes in Seven Lakes State Park: Big Seven, Little Seven, Dickinson, Mud, Spring and Sand Lake. Big Seven and the original Little Seven Lakes were dammed and flooded to form one large 70 acre lake, currently known as Big Seven, while a former walleye pond was renamed Little Seven. One more lake has been purchased by the park and will eventually be improved, and the park will live up to its name once again.

A pleasant beach and picnic site are on the northeast shore of Big Seven Lake. A long winding drive from the park entrance with a scenic overlook on the way leads to a huge meadow which is used as a hot air balloon launching site. The meadow is also used for special events - a vintage car show was in progress on the day of our visit. Picnic tables and grills are on the lawn closer to the beach.

The beach itself is 800 feet long but only 30 feet wide. The sand is very gravelly and has a high dirt content. The buoyed swimming area extends the entire length of the beach and has the same gravel floor as the beach. Canoes, rowboats and paddleboats are available for rental at the beach concession stand. Motorboats are permitted at no wake speeds. A large treed island is visible from the beach and is intriguing to paddle around. Full facilities are offered, including an amusing concession which calls itself the Wild Horse Yacht Club. It sells toys and beach supplies as well as snacks. A play structure, new in 1997, is located at the south end of the beach. Back from the beach is a sand volleyball court.

Two large picnic shelters with electricity and restrooms are available for rental, and an unimproved shelter is available at Dickinson Lake. This lively park hosts special events such as a hot air balloon festival, a "Monster Beach Bash" in July, and interpretive nature programs throughout the summer. But mostly what we found at this northern Oakland County beach were families having fun.

ABOUT THE PARK: A modern 76-site campground with its own beach on Sand Lake draws visitors to this 1,400-acre park in Fenton. Fishing is available at all six lakes with trout, walleye, panfish and bass the primary catches. Ramps at Big Seven and Dickinson lakes allow entry for electric motored boats. Three bicycle/foot trails from 1½ miles to more than two miles wind around Big Seven and Dickinson Lakes. Two foot trails, the Dickinson Trail and the nature trail loop, are under a mile each. Ice fishing, snowmobiling, and cross-country skiing are offered in winter, and hunting is permitted in season.

FEES: Daily $4, Annual $20, Senior Citizen Annual $5

DIRECTIONS: I-75 to exit 101 (Grange Hall Road) and head west to Fish Lake Road. Turn right (north) on Fish Lake Road

BEACH FINDER

PARK NAME	DELORME	UNIVERSAL
Seven Lakes State Park	pg. 41, B4	map 63, E1

to the park entrance.

FURTHER INFORMATION: Seven Lakes State Park, 2220 Tinsman Road, Fenton MI 48430 (810) 634-7271

18 Sterling State Park

Big boats and big water characterize Sterling State Park, the only Michigan state park on Lake Erie.

Entering the park, one is confronted by the less than scenic view of the twin smokestacks of a Detroit Edison coal-burning facility. At the lake, the cooling towers of the Fermi Nuclear Plant belch in the distance. That said, the mile and a quarter natural sand beach more than compensates for the above. The sand is soft and fine, sprinkled through with wood debris. The shoreline of firm wet sand lends itself for walking, but take note of the

shell fragments along the shore as some, especially the zebra mussels, can be sharp.

A gauntlet of shells and then stones must be crossed before hitting the soft sand at the lake's bottom, so folks with sensitive feet may want to wear beach shoes. The unguarded swimming area is buoyed and extends almost the entire length of the beach. The surf is playful - generally wavy and changeable, complete with sandbars and mild currents. High bacteria levels have been an occasional problem at Sterling, but anti-pollution measures and constant monitoring assure swimmers that the water is safe.

A rocky point forms a cove at the southern end of the beach, and there the sand is thick with crushed zebra mussel shells. At the north end, an expensive array of boats bob at anchor. Facilities include a small snack bar and four restroom buildings. Two volleyball nets are set up at the south end of the beach, and four sets of traditional swings and slides are available for children. Some picnic tables are scattered along the beach, and tables and grills adorn the lawn area. Accessible from the north end of the lawn is a paved walkway which runs along the Monroe Harbor Diked Containment Area, then curves around deeper into Lake Erie. For strolling or fishing, this scenic trail is definitely worth exploring.

ABOUT THE PARK: This extremely popular park is outstanding for its birdwatching and fishing opportunities. Established in 1935 to protect Michigan wetlands, this 1,000-acre park includes two lagoons, a creek and a great lake. Birders can find specimens as diverse as herons, egrets, terns, and even osprey. While walleyes are the most popular game fish in the park, anglers can also pull perch, bass, crappie and catfish from the lake and the lagoons, which sport four small fishing piers. Boaters can access Lake Erie from a large boat launch, which has space for 320 cars.

The park also contains a 288-site modern campground, which is in an open meadow with little shade. For hiking, there is a 2.6-mile trail surrounding a marsh, with an observation tower along the way for nature study. The trail is also open for cross-country skiing during the winter.

FEES: Daily $4, Annual $20, Senior Citizen Annual $5

DIRECTIONS: From Detroit, take I-75 south to exit 15 (Dixie Highway). Head east (left) off of the freeway to the park entrance on the right.

BEACH FINDER

PARK NAME	DELORME	UNIVERSAL
Sterling State Park	pg. 25, A6	map 58, G11

FURTHER INFORMATION: Sterling State Park, 2800 Park Road, Route 5, Monroe MI 48161 (313) 289-2715

19 Stony Creek Metropark

Stony Creek Metropark, at 4,461 acres, is the largest of the metroparks. At its center lies Stony Creek Lake, which was created by damming Stony Creek at its north and south ends. This scenic 500-acre lake provides fishing year-round and boating of the quiet variety, as a 10 mph speed limit discourages fast motorboats. Canoes, rowboats and paddleboats, which can be rented at the Mt. Vernon picnic area, mix with sailboats, pontoons and fishing trawlers. A boat launch with 150 parking spaces is available.

The park provides two guarded swimming beaches, Baypoint and Eastwood.

BAYPOINT BEACH

The babe and hunk factor is high at stylish Baypoint Beach. While Eastwood Beach was set up to attract families with children, the park's original beach, Baypoint, is the gathering place for bikini clad singles.

A wide, sloping lawn leads from the parking lot to the sandy beach. The day use area does not provide picnic tables or grills (fires are not allowed), so picnicking groups are relegated to the numerous picnic areas within the park, and Baypoint's lawn is covered with blankets full of sunbathers. The beach itself, at 250 yards long by 100 feet wide, is generously sized with sand that is soft yet mixed with small stone chips.

Swimming at the guarded beach is confined to roped areas. There are three guard towers and swim sections, but the third section is rarely opened. Floats are confined to the first section and a narrow "over four feet deep" section is roped off separately. On busy days this confined swimming makes one feel like a sardine in a can. The water, however, is clear and free of plant debris.

There is a full basketball court near one end of the lawn and a sand volleyball court at the other end. The boat rental concession at the Mt. Vernon picnic area is within walking distance of the beach. The concession stand is efficient, with food provided by Elias Brothers. A separate stand sells rafts, t-shirts, towels and the like as well as renting one-speed 20-inch and 26-inch bicycles. The west/southwest wooded view is serene, with a noticeable lack of noisy powerboats and Jet Skis. More hubbub is provided by boom boxes and loud car radios from the crowd at this lively beach.

EASTWOOD BEACH

Eastwood Beach is almost a twin to its sister around the lake. The beach is of similar size and sand quality; the swimming area is also cordoned off and guarded. However, the northwest direction of the beach is not as conducive to sunbathing as is Baypoint's west/southwest exposure.

More families are attracted to Eastwood, and a play area with four climbing structures sits on the lawn. There are also a sand volleyball court and a full court basketball area near the parking lot. An added attraction near the beach is a 20 station fitness trail with ¾-mile, one-mile, and 1¾ mile trails for all ages to explore. An attractive concession stand and patio are next to a bike rental and store.

Both beaches have separate changing rooms with indoor heated showers, and both are paved to the beach for handicapped accessibility.

ABOUT THE PARK: Stony Creek abounds in diverse recreational opportunities. An 18-hole, par 72 golf course is open to the public (810 -781-9166) and a 9-hole disc-golf course is near the Lakeview picnic area. A boat ramp has room for 10 simultaneous launchings, and summer and winter boat storage is available for rental. Pike, walleye, smallmouth bass, bluegills and perch in Stony Creek Lake make fishing popular. Overnight group camping is available, and a nature center with labeled nature trails is open all year.

Winter activities include hills for sledding and tobogganing, ice fishing, cross-country skiing with marked trails and a rental equipment center, and ice skating rinks with a heated restroom and concession building.

FEES: Weekdays $2, Weekends and holidays $3, Annual $15, Senior annual $8, Wednesdays free.

DIRECTIONS: From M-59, take Rochester Road north to Avon Road. Take Avon Road east to Dequindre Road, then take Dequindre north to 24 Mile Road. Take 24 Mile east to Shelby Road, then head north to the park entrance.

BEACH FINDER

PARK NAME	BEACH NAME	DELORME	UNIVERSAL
Stony Creek Metropark	Baypoint Beach	pg. 42, C2	map 50, K2 map 63, J2
Stony Creek Metropark	Eastwood Beach	pg. 42, C2	map 50, K2 map 63, J2

FURTHER INFORMATION: Stony Creek Metropark, 4300 Main Park Road, Shelby Township MI 48316. (810) 781-4242 or (800) 477-7756.

Stony Creek
Metropark

20 Waterloo Recreation Area

A bit of advice when visiting the beach at Big Portage Lake: Don't haul too many items from your car, for it's a mighty long trek from the parking lot to the lake!

The immense Waterloo Recreation Area, which covers almost 20,000 acres and contains nearly 50 lakes, has only one swimming beach, located at Big Portage Lake on the west side of the park. Also servicing a nearby campground of 194 modern sites, this day use area is enormously popular and draws a large and boisterous crowd. A long expanse of lawn slopes to the lake from the bathhouse/concession building.

Most of the grills and picnic tables are close to the beach, but they aren't supplied in over-abundance considering their heavy usage. Picnickers may want to climb the hill at the park's northwest side, which also supplies tables and grills. This wooded area affords an attractive view of the lake, a kids' swing set and its own bathhouse with restrooms.

The air was thick with cotton from the large cottonwood trees that grow close to the beach on the day that we visited. The 600 by 70 foot beach has hard-packed sand that is not especially soft, but is likewise not rocky. The buoyed swim area is as long as the beach - generously sized for a quiet day but jam-packed on a busy weekend. Motorboats and Jet Skis roared by, causing waves for kids to play in but certainly adding to the noisy, hectic atmosphere. Boats are moored at either side of the lake, and canoes, rowboats (with or without motors), paddleboats, tubes and "fun islands" are available for rental at the concession stand. The beach concession also doubles as the campground store, carrying t-shirts and souvenirs as well as picnic and camping items. Booths are available for dining in, and the store will even deliver pizza to the campsites. An especially welcomed convenience is a coin-operated air hose for inflating rafts and tubes.

South of the lake parking lot is the entrance to the Dry Marsh Nature Trail, a half mile numbered trail which winds through woods and marshland. You'll see black cherry, black oak, quaking and largetooth aspen, red maple and junipers as well as marshland left by ice-age glaciers. A hike along the trail makes a nice break from the beach.

For anglers, bass and panfish are abundant in the lake and there is a fishing pier available, but it is not visible from the beach. There is no paved path from the bathhouse to the lake, which could be difficult for wheelchair access.

ABOUT THE PARK: Winding through two counties and intertwined with private land, there are six exits off of I-94 leading to this massive state park, the largest in the Lower Peninsula. Four campsites are offered, with Sugarloaf and Big Portage featuring modern facilities and Green Campsite and a special horsemen's campground remaining rustic. A tent camping area for youth groups is available at Big Portage Lake. The Mill Lake Outdoor Center features two units, each with four heated sleeping cabins with restrooms, a lodge with a kitchen and dining room, and an infirmary, crafts cabin and classroom in the "A" unit. The center may be rented by calling (734) 475-8307.

Twenty-five miles of bridle trails and over more than 30 miles of hiking trails wander through fields of wildflowers and wonderful birdwatching areas. Dedicated backpackers may want to tackle the forty-six mile long Waterloo-Pickney trail, which begins in Waterloo Park and ends at Silver Lake in the Pickney Recreation Area. Seven short hiking trails are located near the Gerald E. Eddy Geology Center, located in the southeast corner of the park, which features Michigan rocks, minerals, crystals, and information on geology and natural history. The Geology Center can be reached from exit 157 off I-94.

Fishermen have access to 17 lakes, with an improved boat launch on Big Portage Lake and unimproved ramps, walk-in access or fishing piers on the others. Bass, pike, panfish, trout and bluegill are frequent catches. Hunting is available in season in most of the park. Winter activities include ice fishing, snowmobiling, and cross-country skiing on eight miles of marked trails.

FEES: Daily $4, Annual $20, Senior Citizen Annual $5

DIRECTIONS: From I-94, take exit 147 (Race Road). Turn right on Race Road, then right on Seymour Lake Road to the park entrance.

BEACH FINDER

PARK NAME	DELORME	UNIVERSAL
Waterloo Recreation Area	pg. 31, B7	map 38, K2

FURTHER INFORMATION: Waterloo Recreation Area,16345 McClure Road, Route 1, Chelsea MI 48118 (734) 475-8307

Waterloo Recreation Area

21 New Buffalo Beach

They call it "Harbor Country," eight communities that form the gateway to the beautiful western coast of Michigan: Michiana, Grand Beach, New Buffalo, Union Pier, Lakeside, Harbert, Sawyer, and Three Oaks. Along with water related pursuits, this area is a hub for antique collectors. Shop after shop of antiques and collectibles line the Red Arrow Highway.

Just north of the Indiana border is charming New Buffalo, whose bed and breakfasts are now sharing space with fancy new condo developments. The New Buffalo Harbor Navigation Project offers a lovely marina next to a spacious city beach. Sit on the beach and watch the boats cruise slowly through the channel as the sun sets, and lower your blood pressure.

The beach is about a quarter mile long, with fine sand that coarsens slightly towards the waterline and has polished stones at the shore. The swimming area is buoyed and runs the length of the beach. Two lifeguard stands are staffed. There's a volleyball net near the back of the beach and a wooden playscape for kids. A small concession building contains the bathhouse.

Climbing the dunes too daunting? Good size dunes rise up behind the beach and winding stairs provide an accessible dunewalk. Sand wheelchairs are available. A jetty extends along the channel, but it is an uneven jumble of stone and is not recommended for casual strolling. As the first Michigan beach out-of-state visitors may come across, New Buffalo Beach makes a good first impression.

FEES: $5

DIRECTIONS: Take exit 1 off of I-94, turn right to downtown New Buffalo. Take Whitaker Street straight to the beach.

BEACH FINDER

PARK NAME	DELORME	UNIVERSAL
New Buffalo Beach	pg. 18, B1	map 11, A8

FURTHER INFORMATION: New Buffalo Parks Dept., 222 West Buffalo, New Buffalo, MI 49117 (616) 469-1500

22 Warren Dunes State Park

Rounding the bend after entering this state park, the visitor is greeted by a jaw-droppingly large dune known as Tower Hill. All day long children trudge up its sandy sides, then race back down at breakneck speeds. Warren Dunes, along Lake Michigan just north of the Indiana border, attracts visitors from Indiana and Illinois as well as Michigan. Signs are even posted to remind out of state guests that Michigan is in the eastern time zone. Crowded it gets, but this popular beach is capable of handling the crowds, boasting 2½ miles of prime Lake Michigan shoreline. Walk north to where the beach tapers to a strip bordered by dune grass and the crowds are less intense.

The wide beach has clean, fine sand that hardens just enough at the shoreline to make it perfect for strolling. The generous buoyed swim area extends the entire length of the beach. Picnic areas are located away from the beach, as is a rental picnic shelter. Three bathhouses are available, although only the centrally located facility is open unless crowds warrant. If the south parking lot opens, a second concession stand will also become operational. The main concession building also houses a small shop which sells T-shirts and beach supplies. Two patios are provided for chowing down those hot dogs and fries.

For those with special needs beach wheelchairs with oversized tires are available free of charge. Five volleyball courts are near the back of the beach. The park hosts "adventure programs" with park naturalists conducting slide shows, beach walks, sky watches and dune hikes weekly throughout the summer. As

Warren Dunes is located at the furthest end of the eastern time zone, Beach Freaks will appreciate the seemingly endless days of glorious sun.

ABOUT THE PARK: Warren Dunes is a spectacular introduction to the Lake Michigan coastline. This 1,950-acre park features rugged dunes that rise 240 feet above the lake. You'll find sand cherries, wild grape and sasafras trees on the beach dunes, while oaks, maples and pines rise onto mature dunes further from the beach. Six miles of hiking trails, including a one-mile marked interpretive trail, are also used for cross-country skiing. Snowmobiling and hunting are permitted in season.

180 modern dune campsites and 122 semi-modern sites are available. The semi-modern sites sit on a former parking lot, so although they are next to the beach and even on the sand, they are unshaded and have the feeling of, well, a parking lot. Three mini-cabins with electricity may also be rented.

FEES: Daily $4, Annual $20, Senior Citizen Annual $5

DIRECTIONS: I-94 to exit 16 at Bridgeman. South on the Red Arrow Highway two miles to the park entrance.

BEACH FINDER

PARK NAME	DELORME	UNIVERSAL
Warren Dunes State Park	pg. 18, A2	map 11, B6

FURTHER INFORMATION: Warren Dunes State Park, 12032 Red Arrow Highway, Sawyer MI 49125 (616) 426-4013

Warren Dunes
State Park

23 Weko Beach Park

Continuing up the coast from Warren Dunes is a delightful beach and campground in the city of Bridgeman. Weko Beach actually connects to the narrow sliver of beach that makes up the north end of Warren Dunes, then widens to form this half-mile long, 250-foot-wide public beach.

The sand is silky fine and clean, the Lake Michigan surf gently wavy. The only thing marring the view of the vast horizon is a concrete water intake, which sits like the conning tower of a sunken submarine in the center of the swimming area. But the intake predates the beach, so it's there to stay. A lifeguard watches over the buoyed swimming area, which runs the length of the beach.

Behind the beach is a convenient boardwalk with benches and interpretive signs that explain dune wildlife and ecology. Dunes rise on either side of the beach, with winding stairs leading up to scenic vistas. The attractive beach house houses a snack bar, sundry shop, and large game room with a variety of video games and a couple of pool tables.

Two volleyball nets are on the beach, and the facilities are handicapped accessible. To the north of the beachhouse is a small picnic area with a few tables and grills. A boat landing at the north end of the beach is used for launching catamarans and Jet Skis. A 72-site campground with 20 primitive and 52 modern sites is tucked behind the dunes.

FEES: $4 weekdays, $5 weekends

DIRECTIONS: From I-94, take exit 16. Go left at the traffic light to Lake Street. Take Lake Street to the beach entrance.

BEACH FINDER

PARK NAME	DELORME	UNIVERSAL
Weko Beach Park	pg. 18, A2	map 11, B6

FURTHER INFORMATION: Weko Beach Park, 5327 Lake Street, Bridgeman, MI 49106 (616) 465-3406

24 Silver Beach County Park

A fascinating history is connected with this gleaming park at the mouth of the St. Joseph River. A popular steamboat stop for Chicagoans in the 1880s, the park became known for its dance halls and ballrooms during the 1920s. It evolved into an amusement park with rollercoasters and Ferris wheels in the '40s and '50s, but began a slow deterioration during the next two decades. The park closed in 1970 and was purchased by Berrien County in 1990. Extensive renovation throughout the '90s created a terrific facility in the heart of St. Joseph.

A wide sidewalk with benches and decorative street lamps separates the parking lot from the gently sloping beach. The half-mile-long, 300-foot-wide beach has soft, fine, natural sand with some evidence of zebra mussels by the shoreline. Volleyball is king here, with 15 courts (three on the beach) and annual volleyball tournaments. Three lifeguards watch over the 1,600 foot long buoyed swimming area.

A food concession sits right on the sand, with a separate concession for ice cream. Two modern playscapes beckon kids to clamber among bridges, slides and tunnels. Separate bathhouses are available for men and women, and outdoor showers are provided for rinsing. Boats cruise by a picturesque fishing pier and lighthouse to the north. All in all, it's a little bit of Lake Michigan heaven in the city.

FEES: $5

DIRECTIONS: Located in downtown St. Joseph at the corner of Lake and Park Street.

BEACH FINDER

PARK NAME	DELORME	UNIVERSAL
Silver Beach County Park	pg. 26, D3	map 11, C4

FURTHER INFORMATION: Berrien County Parks Commission, Berrien County Courthouse, St. Joseph MI 49085 (616) 983-7111

Erosion and encroaching dunes narrow Van Buren's mile-long beach.

25 Van Buren State Park

We immediately noticed something different about this state park just south of the city of South Haven. The sand is soft, fine...and black! Magnatite, a naturally occuring mineral that causes the dark streaks in hard-packed sand by the water's edge is in abundance, so much so that in some spots this layer of black sand goes more than six inches deep. Also visible near the water's edge is red sand, which is hematite, another mineral found on Lake Michigan's shores. The high concentration of these minerals make this one of the more visually interesting beaches to visit. Water's movement brings out these mineral deposits, so the amount of visible red and black sand varies from year to year.

In 1997 high water levels, encroaching dunes and erosion had narrowed the mile-long Van Buren beach to less than a sliver in spots, and at its widest point the beach measured only 100 feet. The beach is bordered by grass and tree covered dunes. The long unguarded swimming area is buoyed, and has a rocky entrance before reaching the sandy bottom.

The Drake picnic area lies between the parking lot and the beach, so be prepared for a fairly long hike. The picnic area has tables, grills, a playground and a volleyball net. A small bathhouse is near the parking lot. The beach walkway is paved and the restrooms are handicapped accessible. Closer to the beach is a larger bathhouse with a concession stand, snack and pop machines, and restrooms and changing rooms. To the north in the distance is a view of South Haven, to the south lies the

Palisades Nuclear Plant - not the prettiest scene, but it's nestled into the dunes and isn't too intrusive.

ABOUT THE PARK: This over 400 acre park features a 220-site modern campground. A largely undeveloped park, hikers can make their own trails along the shores, dunes and woods. Some of the park is open for hunting, with deer and squirrel popular in season. There are no marked trails, but adventurous snowmobilers and cross-country skiers can set off on their own.

FEES: Daily $4, Annual $20, Senior Citizen Annual $5

DIRECTIONS: From South Haven, take the Blue Star Highway south to Ruggles Road. Turn right (west) on Ruggles to the park entrance.

BEACH FINDER

PARK NAME	DELORME	UNIVERSAL
Van Buren State Park	pg. 26, B4	map 80, E1

FURTHER INFORMATION: Van Buren State Park, 23960 Ruggles Road, South Haven MI 491090 (616) 637-2788

26 South Beach

An unusual phenomenon sometimes occurs on the eastern shore of Lake Michigan, especially at the beaches of South Haven. Westerly winds create waves large enough to surf upon, and the Eastern Surfing Association actually has a Great Lakes district. So although it is the rare Michiganian who owns a surf board, watch for those western breezes to catch a wave with a belly board, raft or your own body.

The southern sister of the twin beaches surrounding the South Haven pier is South Beach, a half-mile curving stretch in downtown South Haven. 250 feet deep at its widest point, this generous beach is popular with families. The shallow, buoyed swimming area is protected by four lifeguards. The north end of the beach is highlighted by a long pier used for strolling and fishing, and is capped by the South Haven Pierhead Lighthouse. Boats cruise the South Haven Harbor channel towards two marinas nearby.

A pay parking lot is located at the north end of the beach (it's on the honor system, but unpaid cars will be ticketed), and there is also free street parking towards the south end. A covered pavilion, modern accessible bathhouse with an outside shower and a concession are also at the north end. A wooden ramp to the water makes the north end handicapped accessible. Swings and slides and a scattering of picnic tables are provided.

The sand quality is excellent - fine and clean, with a clear shoreline at the north end that turns pebbly in the south. The long

shoreline makes for a great summer afternoon stroll.

FEES: $5 parking fee in lot, some parking meters and on-street parking

DIRECTIONS: From the intersection of U.S. 31 and I-196 , take business loop 196 /Phoenix Street west to Broadway. Turn left (south) on Broadway two blocks to Michigan Ave. Turn right (west) on Michigan to Indiana Avenue. Turn left (south) on Indiana to Erie Avenue. Turn right (west) on Erie four blocks to the beach.

BEACH FINDER

PARK NAME	DELORME	UNIVERSAL
South Beach	pg. 27, A4	map 80, E1

FURTHER INFORMATION: Lakeshore Convention and Visitors Bureau, 415 Phoenix Street, South Haven MI 49090 (616) 637-5252

SOUTH HAVEN
RIVERFRONT

27 North Beach

The northern branch of South Haven's twin beaches is similar in character to the southern. A generous 250 feet deep with soft, fine, clean sand, this smaller beach extends about a quarter of a mile. Three lifeguards watch the long, buoyed swim area. The South Haven Pier is also accessible from this beach.

Swings, slides and some picnic tables are near the back of the beach, and a concession/restroom building is at the north end. Several volleyball courts are set up on the beach, but nets must be rented at the concession building. A wooden ramp extends to the sand for accessibility.

The shoreline turns stony midway down the beach, as does the water's entrance. The best shoreline is located at the middle of the beach.

FEES: $5 parking fee, some parking meters and on-street parking

DIRECTIONS: From the intersection of U.S. 31 and I-196, take business loop 196/Phoenix Street west to Broadway. Turn right on Broadway and follow the curve to the left which becomes Dykeman. Take Dykeman a half mile west to North Shore Drive. Turn left on North Shore to Avery. Turn right on Avery to the beach.

BEACH FINDER

PARK NAME	DELORME	UNIVERSAL
North Beach	pg. 27, A4	map 80, E1

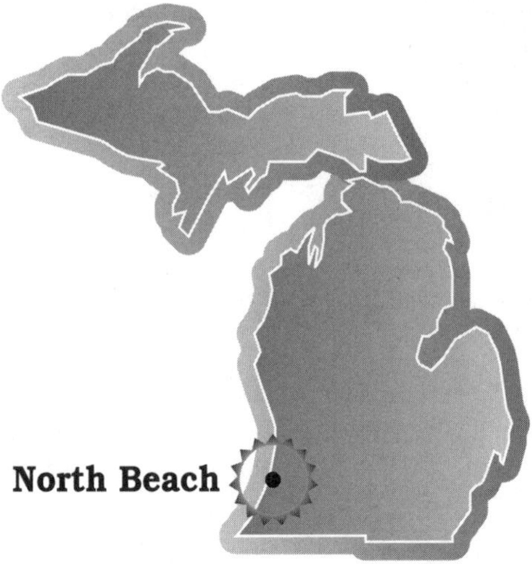
North Beach

28 West Side Park

Slightly off the beaten path between Saugatuck and Holland is a nice county park called West Side. The park offers hilly terrain with lots of picnic tables and grills, two covered pavilions and a fenced playground. There are also swings closer to the beach and, built down a hill, a long, fast, bumpy slide which had kids squealing in delight.

A steep flight of wooden stairs leads down heavily wooded low dunes to the beach. The narrow 25-foot by 500-foot-long beach is protected from inland breezes by a curtain of trees which grow right up to the sand and partially shade it during the morning hours. The soft tan sand is sprinkled with stones and driftwood. The shoreline and water's entrance are heavily pebbled and some excellent fossils can be found. Swimming in the blue Lake Michigan surf is unrestricted and unguarded. There are handicapped accessible restrooms in the park but no wheelchair access to the beach.

Butterflies abound at this peacefully secluded, uncrowded natural beach.

FEES: None

DIRECTIONS: From Holland, Take I-196 to exit 34 (Fennville). Go right one block to Lakeshore Drive. Turn left on Lakeshore to the park entrance.

BEACH FINDER

PARK NAME	DELORME	UNIVERSAL
West Side Park	pg. 35, D5	map 3, C15

FURTHER INFORMATION: Allegan County Parks Dept., 113 Chestnut, Allegan MI 49010 (616) 673-0378

29 Douglas Beach

We counted. There are 97 winding, wooden, precarious steps leading steeply down the face of a dune to Douglas Beach. The hike is broken up by landings with benches and hand railings. The sound of the crashing Lake Michigan surf below is enticing and the beach is... the size of a postage stamp.

The tiny 300-foot-long by 100-foot-wide beach sandwiched between private property has everything going for it but size - soft sand, crashing waves and a beautiful view of the Saugatuck dunes to the north.

There are two picnic tables and grills next to the dirt parking lot, which has room for about a dozen cars. A bathhouse is the only other amenity. But you will envy the gorgeous homes up and down Lakeshore Drive, and if you don't mind climbing the stairs it's one of the best spots for a photo opportunity of the Saugatuck dunes from the shoreline.

FEES: None

DIRECTIONS: From I-196, take exit 41 to the Blue Star Highway. Take the Blue Star Highway to Ferry Street in Douglas. Take Ferry to Center Street. Turn left on Center to Lakeshore Drive. Take Lakeshore right half a block to the beach.

BEACH FINDER

PARK NAME	DELORME	UNIVERSAL
Douglas Beach	pg. 35, C5	map 3, C14

FURTHER INFORMATION: Village of Douglas, 47 W. Center St., Douglas MI 49629 (616) 857-1438

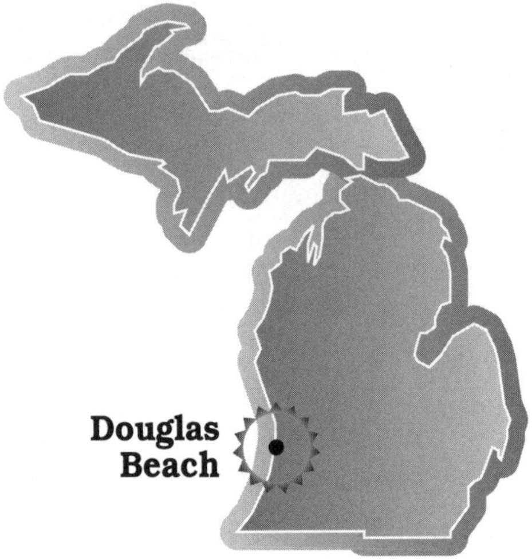

Activities abound at award-winning Oval Beach.

30 Oval Beach

An upscale crowd graces Oval Beach in the tony tourist haven of Saugatuck. Oval Beach has been named one of the best beaches in the country by MTV and one of the 25 best beaches in the world by the Conde Nast Traveler. This ⅛ of a mile long beach features first-rate, clean fine sand with a sprinkling of polished stones at water's edge and entrance. The buoyed and guarded swimming area runs the length of the beach but is only about 200 feet wide. The day we visited the clear, calm Lake Michigan water deepened rapidly but then turned shallow and warm from a sand bar.

Parking lot games and a sand sculpture contest were proceeding with enthusiasm at this lively beach. A boardwalk leads from the parking lot to a concession that offers fat-free selections along with more standard fare. A hot dog cart was set up at the north end of the beach. Restrooms are handicapped accessible but there is no ramp to the beach.

The north end of Oval Beach leads to a privately owned stretch of sand that can be accessed for a $3 fee ($5 on weekends). This private beach is a favorite of the gay community.

FEES: $5 weekdays, $8 weekends, $10 for RV's more than 17 feet long

DIRECTIONS: From I-196, take exit 41 to the Blue Star

Highway. Head west into Douglas to Center Street. Turn right on Center to Ferry Street. Turn right on Ferry and back into Saugatuck where the street is called Park. Turn left at the Oval Beach sign onto Perryman Street to the beach.

BEACH FINDER

PARK NAME	DELORME	UNIVERSAL
Oval Beach	pg. 35, C5	map 3, C14

FURTHER INFORMATION: City of Saugatuck, 102 Butler Street, Saugatuck MI 49453 (616) 857-2603

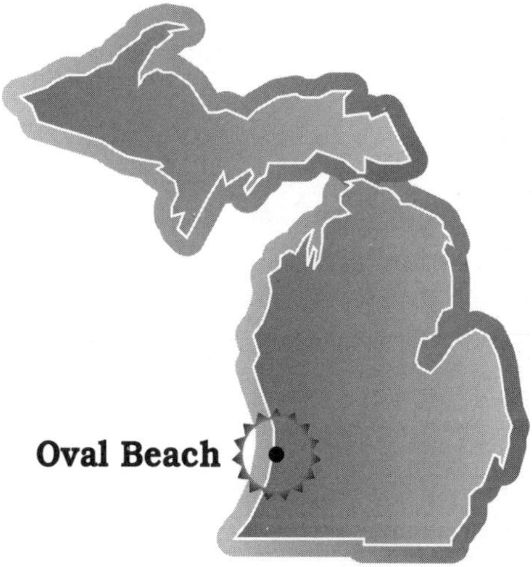

The view is spectacular at little Laketown Township Park.

31 Laketown Township Park

There are two ways to get to the beach at Laketown Township Park south of Holland - both of them over the dunes. We're talking DUNES here, towering mountains of sand that are beautiful to see and a challenge to conquer.

A sandy path directly over the dunes from the 10 car parking lot can be traversed, and this is the easiest route to the beach. The other route involves hundreds of steps, with benches along the way for catching your breath. The stairs are the best way to return from the beach or to catch the view, especially at sunset. Is the arduous climb worth the effort? Yes, for spectacular natural vistas, exquisitely fine sand and unrestricted Lake Michigan swimming - just about all the requirements for a Beach Freak. The beach, however, is small - only 250-feet-long by 50-feet-wide, bounded on both ends by private property. Luckily the small parking lot discourages overcrowding.

One outhouse is the only amenity. This park is the site of a cooperative project with the Rose Lake Plant Materials Center to find solutions to prevent erosion along the shores and dunes of the Great Lakes region. The beach pea, a legume found on sandy shores, has been reestablished at this site, and its purple flowers can be seen at a marker just off the parking lot. This site is also known as Green Mountain Beach.

If you are in good physical condition and appreciate the seclusion of a hidden jewel, pare your gear down to the basics and enjoy.

FEES: None

DIRECTIONS: From Holland, take I-196 south to exit 41. Go right (west) one block to 64th street. Turn right (north) on 64th to 142nd Street. Turn left on 142nd Street, which dead-ends at the park.

BEACH FINDER

PARK NAME	DELORME	UNIVERSAL
Laketown Township Park	pg. 35, C5	map 3, C13

FURTHER INFORMATION: Laketown Township, A-4338 Beeline Road, Holland MI 49424 (616) 355-3050

32 Holland State Park

'Expansive' best describes the beach at Holland State Park, eight miles west of Holland. Everything about it is big - big beach, big swimming area, big views. The beach of delicious, clean sugar sand is 1,800 feet long and so wide your feet will get tired by the time you reach the shoreline. The swimming area is as long as the beach with tall buoys marking its generous boundaries.

A channel connects Lake Michigan with neighboring Lake Macatawa, and a jetty alongside the channel is made for strolling and watching the boats cruise slowly into Holland Harbor. A limestone marker notes the harbor's beginnings in 1847 and the connecting of the two lakes in 1859 which, by the turn of the century, spurred business and resort expansion. The "Big Red" lighthouse, built in 1907, is to the south and views of wooded dunes and upscale condo development are to the north.

Picnic tables, grills and volleyball nets are on a sandy area off of the large parking lot, and a wheelchair ramp at the north end leads all the way to the shore. The concession, the Holland Park Cafe, is run by Big Boy Restaurants. Swings and slides are located at each end of the beach. And if someone tells you to "go fly a kite," that's the perfect activity for this wide open, delightfully sandy shore.

ABOUT THE PARK: This busy park offers two modern campgrounds. The Lake Michigan campground is within spitting distance of the lake, but its 147 treeless sites on an asphalt island offer little in the way of privacy. The Lake Macatawa campsite offers 221 grassy sites about half a mile inland. There is a boat launch near this campground which will accommodate boats under 14 feet in length. Fishing is good at both lakes, and catches include trout, salmon, perch and walleyes.

FEES: Daily $4, Annual $20, Senior Citizen Annual $5

DIRECTIONS: From Holland, take U.S. 31 north to Lakewood Blvd. Exit right (west) on Lakewood to the left fork, which is Douglas Avenue. Douglas turns into Ottawa Beach Road, which dead-ends at the beach entrance.

BEACH FINDER

PARK NAME	DELORME	UNIVERSAL
Holland State Park	pg. 35, B5	map 70, C12

FURTHER INFORMATION: Holland State Park, 2215 Ottawa Beach Road, Holland MI 49424 (616) 399-9390

Cut through the tunnel to the beach...

33 Tunnel Park

Don't despair. Although a daunting set of stairs rises up the dunes at Ottawa County's Tunnel Park, just behind the bathhouse is an easy path through the namesake tunnel which leads to an observation deck and a short stairway to the beach.

But if you'd rather enjoy the loftier view, there are 66 stairs on the park side of the dune and more than a hundred on the lake side. Benches and observation decks are located along the way. An open dune face is next to the stairs on the park side, and energetic children were climbing the stairs to the top, then scrambling full-tilt down the sand. However you get there, the beach itself is terrific. Bordered by thick grasses on swelling dunes, this quarter-mile-long by 35-foot-deep beach is composed of grade A, clean sand. The swimming area is buoyed for the length of the beach, and the day of our visit found crashing surf and sand-bars.

...or give your legs a workout on the stairs over the dunes.

The park features tables and grills, an up-to-date children's playground, two rental picnic shelters and four sand volleyball courts. The modern bathhouse and tunnel to the observation deck are handicapped accessible, but there is no accessible entrance to the beach.

Tunnel Park Beach presents a perfect balance between a secluded natural environment and the niceties of civilization.

FEES: $3 Ottawa County resident, $5 non-resident

DIRECTIONS: From Holland, take U.S. 31 north to the Lakewood Boulevard exit. Go right (west) on Lakewood to Lakeshore Drive. Turn left on Lakeshore Drive ½ mile to the park.

BEACH FINDER

PARK NAME	DELORME	UNIVERSAL
Tunnel Park	pg. 35, B5	map 70, C12

FURTHER INFORMATION: Tunnel Park, 66 Lakeshore Drive, Holland MI 49424 (616) 786-9020

34 Kirk Park

In 1856 an Indian boy named Pooneso Kamosey was buried at the top of a lonely sand dune. That sand dune eventually became part of a Boy Scout camp, Camp Kirk. In 1973 Ottawa County purchased the camp, which became Kirk Park, and Pooneso's grave marker can still be seen on top of the dune south of the beach viewing deck.

Ottawa County has another winner with this fine 68-acre park, which features picnic areas, a network of hiking trails and paved trails, including the handicapped accessible South Trail to a viewing deck, two playgrounds and two horseshoe pits. The bathhouse includes a concession stand with a small patio. A lodge which sleeps 24 or seats 50 is available for group rental. The path and boardwalk to the Lake Michigan beach also lead to the Dune Ridge Trail, a steep climb up wooden stairs to an overlook point.

The quarter-mile beachfront is shortened by high water levels and erosion, but the narrow band of sand, only 25 feet deep at its widest point, is still a delight. A-1 sand littered with dried dune grass and a dark shoreline heavy with magnatite lead to a buoyed, generous swimming area. The dunes, rising 200 feet above the shore, are covered with oak, beech and hemlock, while a red pine plantation grows on the east side of the park. Only its undersized shoreline mars the perfection of this lovely site.

FEES: $3 Ottawa County resident, $5 non-resident

DIRECTIONS: From Holland, take U.S. 31 north to Lakewood Blvd. Turn right (north) on Lakeshore Drive to the park.

BEACH FINDER

PARK NAME	DELORME	UNIVERSAL
Kirk Park	pg. 35, A5	map 70, C10

FURTHER INFORMATION: Kirk Park, 9791 Lakeshore Drive, West Olive MI 49460 (616) 847-1240

35 Grand Haven State Park

Stunt kites were soaring and diving on the cloudless day that we visited Grand Haven State Park. The entire 48-acre park consists of sand, including the campground. The beach is roughly ½ mile by 250 feet, a flat expanse of fine yellow sand dotted with pebbles. The buoyed swimming area runs the entire length of the beach.

An attractive, spacious bathhouse offers a sundry and souvenir shop as well as housing a large rental room with picnic tables. The food concession is run by Big Boy and even offers breakfast selections. Indoor as well as patio dining are available. To the north of the bathhouse are several volleyball courts and a nice children's playground. The picnic area consists of two sandy strips in the middle of the parking lot with tables and grills, which is convenient but hardly scenic. Continue north for a stroll along the Grand Haven pier and lighthouse.

An old-fashioned trolley stops at the park entrance and will take you around town for only 25 cents. Grand Haven is known for "the world's largest musical fountain" which performs nightly at dusk during the summer.

ABOUT THE PARK: A state park since 1921, this small park features a 174-site sandy modern campground next to a marvelous beach. The park has no boat launch, but a launch can be found on nearby Harbor Island which gives anglers access to both Lake Michigan and the Grand River, which borders the east side of the park. The Grand Haven pier also provides an excellent opportunity for shore fishing.

FEES: Daily $4, Annual $20, Senior Citizen $5

DIRECTIONS: From Grand Haven, take U.S. 31 to Franklin Avenue. Take Franklin west to Harbor Drive to the park entrance.

BEACH FINDER

PARK NAME	DELORME	UNIVERSAL
Grand Haven State Park	pg. 45, D5	map 70, C9

FURTHER INFORMATION: Grand Haven State Park, 1001 Harbor Ave., Grand Haven MI 49417 (616) 798-3711

36 Grand Haven City Beach

No amenities

A split-rail fence is all that separates Grand Haven's city beach from that of Grand Haven State Park. The beach has the same lovely soft sand extending about ½ mile down the coast, with buoyed swimming along its length. There are no facilities on the beach, but if you don't mind the walk you can use the state park bathhouse or grab a snack at Bill Mar's Restaurant, which is right behind the beach. Parking can be tight, with a small lot and some parallel street parking available. No watercraft or dogs are allowed on the beach.

It's a frugal man's version of the state park.

FEES: None

DIRECTIONS: U.S. 31 to Harbor Drive. West on Harbor Drive to the beach.

BEACH FINDER

PARK NAME	DELORME	UNIVERSAL
Grand Haven City Beach	pg. 45, D5	map 70, C9

FURTHER INFORMATION: Grand Haven Parks Dept., 1120 Jackson, Grand Haven MI 49417 (616) 847-3493

Grand Haven
City Beach

37 North Beach Park

Another of Ottawa County's well-managed parks, North Beach is a nice little getaway just north of Grand Haven in Ferrysburg.

The ¼-mile-long sloping beach has delightfully soft, clean sand and a generous buoyed swimming area that runs the length of the beach. The bathhouse has no concession but does provide beverage and snack machines. Tables and grills line the back of the beach, and a rental pavilion has a wheelchair ramp that runs almost to the water's edge. There's also a volleyball court and a colorful children's playscape. Behind the parking lot are a couple of small staircases with observation platforms.

This is your basic family beach on which to spend a pleasant afternoon.

FEES: $3 Ottawa County resident, $5 non-resident

DIRECTIONS: Take U.S. 31 to the Ferrysburg exit (north of Grand Haven). Take 3rd street west which curves to become 174th Street. Continue to Northshore Drive. Turn left (west) on Northshore. The park is on the right.

BEACH FINDER

PARK NAME	DELORME	UNIVERSAL
North Beach Park	pg. 45, D4	map 70, C9

FURTHER INFORMATION: Ottawa County Parks and Recreation Commission, 414 Washington St., Grand Haven MI 49417 (616) 846-8117

North Beach
Park

38 P. J. Hoffmaster State Park

Nearly three miles of shoreline mark the P.J. Hoffmaster State Park. The beach is beautiful, the sand soft and fine with forested dunes rising up behind and an open dune for scrambling up and running down - better than any playground!

The main section of the beach opens up for roughly a mile before narrowing at either end. Lake Michigan swimming is buoyed at the largest section of the beach. Two bathhouses are off of the parking lot. There is no concession but beverage and snack machines are provided. Behind one bathhouse lies a sandy picnic area with tables and grills.

There are two ways to access the beach — a 30 step staircase with an observation lookout or a sloping dune walk. A mother was negotiating a loaded stroller down the slope with some difficulty - tricky, but possible.

One of Hoffmaster's major attractions is the E. Genevieve Gillette Sand Dune Visitor Center. The center features an 82-seat theater that shows multi-image slide shows and features an exhibit hall, an art gallery and a classroom, all focusing on Michigan's sand dune ecology and the Great Lakes. A dune climb stairway leads from the Visitor Center to observation decks on one of the park's highest dunes.

ABOUT THE PARK: Hoffmaster features a popular 293-site modern campground in a wooded valley, as well as wooded picnic sites and a group rental shelter. Ten miles of hiking trails wind through the park's 1,150 acres and a marked cross-country skiing trail is open during the winter. Bird watchers will find abundant species of shoreline and aquatic birds as well as hawks who soar through the dunes. Snowmobiles and off-road vehicles, however, are not allowed in the park.

FEES: Daily $4, Annual $20, Senior Citizen Annual $5

DIRECTIONS: South from Muskegon, take U.S. 31 to the Pontaluna exit. Head west off the exit on Pontaluna Road to the park entrance.

BEACH FINDER

PARK NAME	DELORME	UNIVERSAL
P.J. Hoffmaster State Park	pg. 45, D4	map 70, C9

FURTHER INFORMATION: P.J. Hoffmaster State Park, 6585 Lake Harbor Road, Muskegon MI 49441 (231) 798-3711

39 Bronson Park

(Norman F. Kruse Park)

One of the most wheelchair accessible dune country parks we've encountered is Bronson Park in Muskegon. A ramping system of hairpin turns winds down a dune face to a platform right on the beach. Even the playground has a wheelchair height "sandbox" for little ones.

The park's name is a bit confusing. Purchased from the Brownson family in 1890, the park was called Bronson Park. In 1994 the park was renamed to honor a benefactor, Norman F. Kruse, but most maps still refer to it as Bronson.

At the entrance, heading right takes you to the main area of the park, with a bathhouse, four rental pavilions with large grills, a small concession cart and a modern playground with lots of colorful apparatus. There's also a dune climb with steep wooden stairs. Turn left to find the parking lot for "Old Bronson Beach" where the handicapped ramping begins. There are also stairs which shorten the length of the route. The beach itself is long and narrow, only 30 feet at its widest point, narrowing to a sliver of sand between the dunes and the surf.

The fine sand was fairly heavy with plant debris (and a bit more human debris than we like to see) although a "fire square" encourages campfire ashes to be contained. The Lake Michigan swimming is wide open, and signs warn of possible currents and riptides. A good cleaning would make this narrow shoreline and fine park a more highly recommended site.

FEES: None

DIRECTIONS: From Muskegon, take U.S. 31 to Sherman Boulevard. Head west on Sherman all the way to its end at the park entrance.

BEACH FINDER

PARK NAME	DELORME	UNIVERSAL
Bronson Park	pg. 44, C4	map 61, B8

FURTHER INFORMATION: Muskegon Department of Leisure Services, 933 Terrace, Muskegon MI 49445 (231) 724-6704

Ride the trolley to popular Marquette Park.

40 Pere Marquette Park

Dunes found south of the city disappear at Pere Marquette Park, a huge local beach in Muskegon. Join the party at this beach which boasts the only authentic beach bar on the Great Lakes. Jalepenos Beach Bar serves food and drinks, and was the site of a Bud Lite volleyball tournament the day of our visit. In fact, volleyball is a major activity at this spacious beach, which holds 35 volleyball courts and hosts regular league play.

The 400-foot-wide, flat beach has clean sugar sand and a clear, curving shoreline that extends a good half mile. Four lifeguards watch over the large buoyed swimming area; swimming is allowed past the guard stands to the south. A pier along the channel to Muskegon Lake, part of the Muskegon Harbor Navigation Project, is located at the north end of the beach for strolling.

The park offers the Pavilion Ice Cream Shop alongside Jalepenos Bar, as well as a bathhouse with a gift and snack shop. A colorful children's playscape and swings are located on both sides of the bathhouse. The park is a stop along the North Beach trolley line, a 25-cent reminder of the 1890s when trolleys were prevalent in Muskegon. Enjoy hot times, summer in the city!

FEES: None

DIRECTIONS: From Muskegon, take U.S. 31 to Sherman Boulevard. West on Sherman to Beach Street. Right (north) on Beach to the park.

BEACH FINDER

PARK NAME	DELORME	UNIVERSAL
Pere Marquette Park	pg. 44, C4	map 61, B7

FURTHER INFORMATION: Muskegon Department of Leisure Services, 933 Terrace Avenue, Muskegon MI 49445 (213) 724-6704

The primal urge to dig is unleashed at Michigan's beaches.

41 Muskegon State Park

With a picturesque view of lighthouses to the south, luscious wooded dunes to the north and east, and the open vista of Lake Michigan to the west, you'd never know that you were just outside an industrial city. And although not as rustically pretty as beaches set within the dunes, the convenience offered by being able to step out of your car and onto the beach can have its advantages.

The day use area of Muskegon State Park offers more than two miles of shoreline on Lake Michigan. This is a wide, flat beach with gorgeous tan sand and a very clean shoreline. The buoyed swimming area is also enormous. A large concession building offers a bathhouse with indoor showers. The park is handicapped accessible all the way from the parking lot to the shoreline. There is a swing set by the concession building.

Tables and grills are set on sandy islands within the large parking lot - conveniently close to your car but not the most attractive place to have a picnic. With numerous activities offered at the state park to take advantage of and miles of shoreline to explore, Muskegon State Park is worth a visit.

ABOUT THE PARK: Established in 1923, the park includes shoreline on Muskegon Lake as well as on Lake Michigan. Three campgrounds, two modern and one semi-modern, are available as are two heated mini-cabins which sleep four. Twelve miles of hiking trails wind through varied terrain, with five miles lighted for cross-country skiing. Other winter activities include ice skating, fishing and a luge run. Snug Harbor on Muskegon Lake offers a lighted boat launch for trailered boats as well as a second launch for small boats. Pier fishing is available at Snug Harbor and along the channel walkway.

FEES: Daily $4, Annual $20, Senior Citizen Annual $5

DIRECTIONS: U.S. 31 north of Muskegon to the M-120 exit to Giles Road. Turn right (west) on Giles to Scenic Drive. Turn left (south) on Scenic to the park entrance.

BEACH FINDER

PARK NAME	DELORME	UNIVERSAL
Muskegon State Park	pg. 44, C4	map 61, B7

FURTHER INFORMATION: Muskegon State Park, 3560 Memorial Drive, North Muskegon MI 49445 (231) 744-4623

A large rental lodge and great camping define rustic Pioneer Park.

42 Pioneer Park

North of Muskegon State Park is a county park called Pioneer. Although its main feature is a modern campground, its 2,200 feet of Lake Michigan shoreline make it a site worth visiting.

The heavily treed park offers table and grills, a large rental lodge with cooking facilities, a picnic shelter and a sandy playground. The handicapped accessible bathhouse is nearer to the campground, so restrooms are a hike from the beach. Special features of the park include basketball, volleyball and tennis

courts, and a softball diamond. The campground offers 213 individual and 27 group campsites with water and electrical hookups.

The beach can be accessed from either a sandy path down a low dune or a set of metal steps. A nice observation deck is at the top of the dunes, as are another wooded deck and porch swing. The natural beach, bordered by dune grass, is about 45 feet at its widest point, narrowing at each end. The sand is soft and fine, and the Lake Michigan swimming is sandy-bottomed and unrestricted by ropes or buoys. Campers especially should take a look at this rustic, woodsy park.

FEES: $2, seasonal $10, senior citizen seasonal $5

DIRECTIONS: From Muskegon, take U.S. 31 north to the Fremont/Big Rapids exit (Route 120). Go south on Route 120 to Giles Road. Head west (right) on Giles to Scenic Drive. Turn west (right) on Scenic to the park entrance ¼ mile on the left.

BEACH FINDER

PARK NAME	DELORME	UNIVERSAL
Pioneer Park	pg. 44, B4	map 61, B7

FURTHER INFORMATION: Pioneer County Park, 1563 N. Scenic Drive, Muskegon MI 49445 (231) 744-3580

Duck Lake flows under Scenic Drive into Lake Michigan.

43 Duck Lake State Park

All the folks we spoke to who were enjoying the unique pleasures of Duck Lake State Park had no idea where they were. They simply spied the beach, pulled over to the side of the road, hauled out the kids and the coolers and began to have fun.

There are two beaches in the park. One is a small indent of sand on Duck Lake with a picnic area behind it. Offered are a rental shelter with tables, including a wheelchair accessible picnic table, and restrooms.

The beach to look for, however, is around Duck Lake on Scenic Drive. Here Duck Lake runs into Lake Michigan, and bathers have the option of swimming in the calm warmth of the inland lake or dodging the waves of the Great Lake. A shallow creek under a bridge on Scenic Drive divides the two lakes and the creek was filled with playing children.

There is street parking along Scenic Drive close to the beach. A parking lot with an outhouse is also accessible from inside the park with a walkway leading back to the beach. The beach itself is lovely, with pure sugar sand backed by both developing fore-dunes and mature forested dunes.

Most of the crowd stays near the shallow waters connecting to Duck Lake, so there's plenty of open space further down the Lake Michigan shoreline, which extends about ½ mile. Swimming is open with polished stones along the shore.

Dogs were everywhere on the unrestricted beach, obviously having as much fun as their owners. If you don't mind the lack of close facilities, the uncommon linking of an inland lake, a Great Lake, and scenic dunes make Duck Lake State Park one you shouldn't miss.

The beach on Duck Lake.

ABOUT THE PARK: This 704-acre park is largely undeveloped save for its two beaches. There is a boat launch on Duck Lake, and anglers can find pike and panfish. Hunting is also permitted in season.

Striking dunes rise up from Lake Michigan.

FEES: Daily $4, Annual $20, Senior Citizen Annual $5

DIRECTIONS: U.S. 31 north of Muskegon to the Lakewood Club exit. Take White Lake Road to Zellar Road. Turn left (south) on Zellar to Michillinda Road. Turn right (west) on Michillinda to the park entrance.

BEACH FINDER

PARK NAME	DELORME	UNIVERSAL
Duck Lake State Park	pg. 44, B3	map 61, B6

FURTHER INFORMATION: Duck Lake State Park c/o Muskegon State Park, 3560 Memorial Drive, North Muskegon MI 49445 (231) 894-8769

44 Meinert Park

Although the facilities are somewhat aged, the beach at Muskegon County's Meinert Park is terrific. A generous ¼ mile long, the soft white sand is first-rate and forested dunes make a beautiful backdrop. The swimming in Lake Michigan is unrestricted by ropes or buoys.

The park offers a small bathhouse, a concession stand, an old-fashioned playground and a small picnic area with tables and grills. There is also an observation platform atop a low dune with benches for viewing. But the lovely beach is the star of this show!

FEES: $3 Daily, $15 Annual

DIRECTIONS: From Muskegon, take U.S. 31 north to the Fruitvale (B-15) exit. Follow B-15 west 1.5 miles to Whitbeck Road. Go right (north) on Whitbeck to Meinert Park Road. Turn left (west) on Meinart to the end of the road and the park entrance.

BEACH FINDER

PARK NAME	DELORME	UNIVERSAL
Meinert Park	pg. 44, A3	map 61, A5

FURTHER INFORMATION: Muskegon County Public Works Dept., 990 Terrace, Muskegon MI 49442 (231) 724-6361

Meinert Park

45 Silver Lake State Park,
Little Sable Point Lighthouse

At the southern edge of Silver Lake State Park, this picture-post-card beach is the site of the Little Sable Point Lighthouse, one of the oldest working lighthouses in Michigan. Built in 1874, the lighthouse was automated in 1954.

You have to walk through the dunes to reach the shoreline, and though not overly steep it is still a bit of an arduous climb. Arduous but beautiful, and the small beach has sand so fine it is of glass-making quality. Dunes rise up around the beach and the brick lighthouse to create a breathtaking scene.

The beach extends about an eighth of a mile by 50-feet, but you can tuck a blanket into numerous places further back into the dunes. The Lake Michigan surf is unbuoyed and delicious. Outhouses are provided. Bring your camera to this one!

ABOUT THE PARK: Silver Lake State Park is synonymous with the word "sand." Half of the 2,675-acre park consists of enormous, mind-boggling dunes. This is the only state park where buggies are allowed on the dunes, and ORV's line up for the privilege of zooming around on the 450-acre Off Road Vehicle Area. Dune hikers have 750 acres which are reserved for pedestrians.

East of the dunes is Silver Lake, which offers a small beach, picnic area and boat launch. Fishing is popular in both Silver Lake and Lake Michigan for bass, brown trout, perch and walleye. Two modern campgrounds by the lake get heavy usage. Hunting is permitted in part of the park in season. Close to the park are arcades, water slides, dune buggy rentals and the famous Mac Woods Dune Rides.

FEES: Daily $4, Annual $20, Senior Citizen Annual $5

DIRECTIONS: From U.S. 31 about 35 miles north of Muskegon, take the Shelby Road exit west. Take Shelby Road to 16th Avenue. Turn right on 16th to Buchanan Road. Turn right on Buchanan to 18th Avenue. Turn left on 18th (B 15) and head north to Silverlake Road. Turn left on Silverlake past Mac Woods Dune Rides and follow as it winds around to the lighthouse parking lot.

BEACH FINDER

PARK NAME	BEACH NAME	DELORME	UNIVERSAL
Silver Lake State Park	Little Sable Point Lighthouse Beach	pg. 54, C2	map 64, A2

FURTHER INFORMATION: Silver Lake State Park, P.O. Box 187, Rt. 1, Mears MI 49436 (231) 873-3083

Silver Lake
State Park

46 Charles Mears State Park

Visitors to the charming village of Pentwater flock to the beach at Mears State Park. The small 50 acre state park's primary feature is its large beach on Lake Michigan, with boating access and a channel to Pentwater Lake.

The wide, flat beach consists of about 1,500 feet of feather soft, fine sand. The buoyed swimming area extends the length of the beach but does not extend very far into the water. A lovely view of Ludington's bluffs and dunes sweeps around to the north, while Pentwater Pier for strolling or fishing is at the south end. Benches line the back of the beach around a bathhouse which features a concession with a covered patio.

Behind the beach is a sandy picnic area with tables and grills, and a traditional playground. A volleyball net is also set up near the back of the beach at the north end. Boats launch at Pentwater Lake then cruise the South Harbor Channel into Lake Michigan past Mears. Boaters and Jet-Skiers are part of the activity at this busy beach.

ABOUT THE PARK: This small park contains a very popular campground, which offers 180 modern sites. Old Baldy, the largest dune in the park, features a half mile trail to the top. Anglers will enjoy fishing off Pentwater Pier in the summer for perch and bass and in the fall for trout and salmon. Late fall finds surf fishermen casting rods from the beach.

FEES: Daily $4, Annual $20, Senior Citizen Annual $5

DIRECTIONS: Take business route M-31 to downtown Pentwater. Go west on Lowell Street to the park entrance.

BEACH FINDER

PARK NAME	DELORME	UNIVERSAL
Charles Mears State Park	pg. 54, B3	map 64, A1

FURTHER INFORMATION: Charles Mears State Park, P.O. Box 370, Pentwater MI 49449 (231) 869-2051

47 Stearns Park

The center of action in the unpretentious resort of Ludington is Stearns Park, where you'll find teenagers cruising the long parking lot, senior citizens playing shuffleboard, and people of all ages turning out at dusk to stroll the pier and watch the sunset.

The beach is outstanding, consisting of 2,500 feet of silky soft, incredibly fine clean sand. The 300-foot-wide beach features six volleyball nets, two bathhouses, and a view of state park land to the north. The bathhouses both contain House of Flavors ice cream concessions, and a building for Jet Ski rentals and a playground are located at the beach's south end. A separate parking lot to the south services a heavily used boat launch.

The day of our visit found barely a ripple in the large buoyed swimming area, which is guarded by two lifeguards. The Ludington Harbor Navigation Project contributes a long pier and the North Pierhead lighthouse at the south end of the beach. Behind the beach and parking lot is a manicured picnic area with tables, grills and 14 shuffleboard courts, with play costing only $1 an hour and free to senior citizens. The Jaycees run a mini-golf course across the street.

The park has a Michigan Historic Site, commemorating the car ferry S.S. Pere Marquette 18, which sunk midway between Ludington and Wisconsin in 1910. A ferry still departs from Ludington today for Manitowoc, Wisconsin.

FEES: None

DIRECTIONS: From downtown Ludington, take Ludington Avenue west until it ends at the park.

BEACH FINDER

PARK NAME	DELORME	UNIVERSAL
Stearns Park	pg. 54, A3	map 53, A15

FURTHER INFORMATION: City of Ludington, 1323 Sherman Avenue, Ludington MI 49431 (231) 845-2517

Ludington State Park offers one of Lake Michigan's most beautiful stretches of shoreline.

48 Ludington State Park

Three distinct beaching choices await the visitor to Ludington State Park. Several miles of shoreline and a wealth of activities make this a can't-miss stop on Michigan's sunset coast.

LAKE MICHIGAN BEACH

The Lake Michigan beach at Ludington State Park is a perfect combination of beautiful sugar sand, Lake Michigan swimming and great facilities. The flat ⅛-mile-long by 150-foot-wide beach has low dunes rising at each end as well as low dunes behind the parking lot. A small playground is near a full-service beach-house, which offers both the Ludington Park Cafe for a more leisurely meal or, in the lower level, The Grill for a quick snack or souvenirs.

Benches line the back of the beach for viewing the boats cruising by or for watching swimmers enjoying the large, buoyed swimming area in the Lake Michigan surf.

HAMLIN LAKE

Michigan's largest artificially created lake, the 5000-acre Hamlin Lake, narrows as it winds past Ludington State Park. The lake was created when the Sable River was dammed 100 years ago during Michigan's lumber boom as a means to float logs to the local mill for sawing. While not as grand as the park's Lake

Michigan beach, Hamlin's calm, warm, shallow water and boating opportunities provide a varied beaching experience.

The east-facing beach has the same high-quality sand as the Lake Michigan beach, but extends only 300 feet in length by 80 feet in width. The buoyed swimming area doesn't extend very far into the lake. Paddle boats, rowboats, canoes and aquacycles may be rented, and a boat launch is also nearby. The bathhouse offers a Big Boy concession stand. Buy food...and bait! The large, sandy picnic area behind the beach has tables, grills and a small playground.

ROADSIDE BEACHES

No amenities

Between Stearns City Park and the state park on route M-116 lie three miles of gorgeous Lake Michigan shoreline and beaches with the softest imaginable sand. Parking is permitted along the roadside, and there are also five pull-offs along the way with limited parking that access paths to the beach.

For Beach Freaks who prefer a natural environment and don't need additional facilities, these roadside beaches are unsurpassed. Bordered by dunes of various configurations, the beachfront varies in size and offers plenty of private coves and nooks in which to settle. The water is crystal clear and inviting. Be sure to honor the natural environment and remove any signs of your visit.

Close to state park facilities and Ludington proper, yet secluded enough to really feel "away from it all," the roadside beaches show the Michigan shoreline at its best.

ABOUT THE PARK: One of the prettiest state parks in Michigan is Ludington, with almost 5,300 acres of sand dunes and shoreline along both a Great and an inland lake. The park features an outstanding trail system, with 11 foot trails winding 18 miles through woods and dunes. There are also 16 miles of cross-country trails and a unique canoe pathway. This pathway provides a guided route of near-shore paddling starting at the

Hamlin Lake canoe livery.

Provided are three modern campsites with 344 sites and a park store. Three mini-cabins designed to sleep four are available to rent. The Great Lakes Visitor Center offers live programs, displays, and special presentations. Anglers can enjoy fishing in Hamlin Lake, Lake Michigan, and the Big Sable River below the Hamlin Dam. Small game and deer hunting is permissible in parts of the park, and cross-country skiing, hiking and ice fishing are popular during the winter months.

FEES: Daily $4, Annual $20, Senior Citizen Annual $5

DIRECTIONS: From Ludington, take Lakeshore Drive north 8 miles. Lakeshore becomes M-116 which ends at the park entrance.

BEACH FINDER

PARK NAME	BEACH NAME	DELORME	UNIVERSAL
Ludington State Park	Hamlin Lake Beach	pg. 64, D3	map 53, A14
Ludington State Park	Lake Michigan Beach	pg. 64, D2	map 53, A14
Ludington State Park	Roadside Beach	pg. 64, D2	map 53, A14

FURTHER INFORMATION: Ludington State Park, P.O. Box 709, M-116, Ludington MI 49431 (231) 843-8671

49 Michigan Recreation Area, Manistee National Forest

Visit the only designated wilderness area in Michigan's lower peninsula and find Beach Freaks' nirvana. The Michigan Recreation Area is part of the Nordhouse Dunes Wilderness in the Manistee National Forest. Hike the 10 miles of trails, camp at the four wooded camping or group camping loops, or backpack into the wilderness. But don't miss the beautiful beach on Lake Michigan.

From the parking lot, steps to the right lead to a long stair climb to an observation deck. Continue down the wooden path to a marvelous natural beach - grade A sand surrounded by rolling dunes and a shoreline that stretches for miles. The blue water is some of the cleanest in Lake Michigan, open for swimming and slightly stony at the shoreline. Located in a large cove, the view of dunes to the north and south is stunning. Not as narrow as other dune beaches, the width reaches 50 feet.

The heavily wooded recreation area has cement islands built in among the trees, each island containing a picnic table and a grill. There's a wooden playscape for kids and outhouses provided. Dogs are allowed on the north end of the shoreline but not on the swimming beach.

Nordhouse Dunes encompasses more than 275,000 acres of dunes along the Michigan shoreline, and are part of the formations which include Ludington State Park and Hamlin Lake. Sit on the bench atop the dune at the head of the beach entrance trail and drink in one of the best views on Michigan's west coast.

FEES: None

DIRECTIONS: From Scottsville (8 miles east of Ludington), Take U.S. 31 north 11.5 miles to Forest Trail. Head west on Forest Trail about eight miles to the Recreation Area on the left.

BEACH FINDER

PARK NAME	DELORME	UNIVERSAL
Michigan Recreation Area Manistee National Forest	pg. 64, D3	map 53, A13

FURTHER INFORMATION: Manistee Ranger Station, 412 Red Apple Road, Manistee MI 49660 (231) 723-2211

50 First Street Beach

Several named parks including Douglas, Rotary and Rocket Park comprise the First Street Beach in Manistee. A complex behind the beach provides covered shelters, tennis courts, a basketball court and two ball fields, as well as a sandy playground with swings shaped like rocket ships.

First Street Beach itself is an eighth-mile long, 300-foot-wide flat expanse with low dunes rising at either end. The sand is of good quality and the sparkling Lake Michigan swimming area is buoyed and guarded. Two volleyball nets are on the beach and a long fishing pier extends into the lake and bends to the north. A traditional playground is located at the back of the beach.

Behind the beach and slightly north is the First Street Beach Launching Facility, with eight docks and room for 16 boats to launch at a time. A food and ice cream concession is across from the boat launch parking lot.

FEES: None

DIRECTIONS: From downtown Manistee, take River Street west. River Street becomes Water Street. Take Water Street to First Street. Turn right (west) on First Street until it ends at the beach.

BEACH FINDER

PARK NAME	DELORME	UNIVERSAL
First Street Beach	pg. 64, C4	map 51, B12

FURTHER INFORMATION: Douglas Park, 110 S. Lakeshore Drive, Manistee MI 49660 (231) 723-4051

51 Fifth Avenue Beach

Wind through the handsome residential complex in Manistee known as Harbor Village to find spacious Fifth Avenue Beach. With a quarter mile of wide, flat sand and about as much narrow shoreline to the north, this beach provides plenty of elbow room.

The tan sand itself is a bit gritty and is scattered through with pebbles and stones. The clear Lake Michigan surf is buoyed and protected by two lifeguards from the beginning of summer through mid-August. The south end of the beach finds a bathhouse, sandy playground, and concession trailer. A small grassy picnic area surrounds a rental log cabin, and nearby are two volleyball nets, two tennis courts and a ball field. Across from the beach is a Coast Guard station, and the Manistee Harbor Navigation Project provides two narrow piers, both of which are available for fishing and one which is capped by the Manistee North Pierhead lighthouse.

FEES: None

DIRECTIONS: From downtown Manistee, take Fifth Avenue (the first street over the bridge) west. Turn right (north) on Monroe Street into Harbor Village. Take Monroe to Lakeshore Drive. Turn left (west) on Lakeshore Drive to the beach.

BEACH FINDER

PARK NAME	DELORME	UNIVERSAL
Fifth Avenue Beach	pg. 64, B4	map 51, B12

Fifth Avenue
Beach

52 Veteran's Memorial Park

Arcadia is a town at the northern edge of Manistee County, and there you'll find a nice little park that leads to a curving stretch of beach around a cove. The park sits above the beach on low dunes, and there's a lookout platform with tables, a playground, a small picnic area and an outhouse. Two sets of steps lead to the beach.

The beach is narrow, with silky soft sand and a pebbly shoreline. If you like, you can hike south around the cove to a jetty and lighthouse. Low forested dunes rise behind the beach, and the swimming in Lake Michigan is unrestricted by ropes or buoys. Veteran's Memorial Park doesn't appear on most maps.

AMENITIES: Restrooms, tables, grills, play area

FEES: None

DIRECTIONS: Take M-22 into Arcadia, head west on Lake Street to the end.

BEACH FINDER

PARK NAME	DELORME	UNIVERSAL
Veteran's Memorial Park	pg. 65, A5	map 51, C9

FURTHER INFORMATION: Arcadia Township Hall, 3422 Lake St., Arcadia MI 49613 (231) 857-4463

Veteran's
Memorial Park

53 Elberta Recreation Area

"Take only pictures, leave only footprints," says the sign at the entrance to the Elberta Recreation Area. This extremely rustic beach borders the south side of the Frankfort Harbor Navigation Project, and the pier along the channel is accessible for fishing or strolling.

The narrow beach extends for miles, with sand that is slightly gritty (and very musical) and wide open Lake Michigan swimming. The view to the north is industrial, the view to the south is of rising distant dunes, but the view behind the beach is spectacular, with forested dunes rising like sentries watching over the lake. Look to the skies for silent sailplanes soaring over the dunes.

One lone, rusty swing and an outhouse building are the only amenities. A wooden walkway, each board engraved with park contributors, leads from the parking lot to the beach. Travel south down the sandy road from the main parking lot and climb over low dunes to get away from the crowd, but be careful not to go too far or you may find your vehicle stuck in the sand.

FEES: None

DIRECTIONS: M-22 north to M-168 west to Frankfort Avenue, which runs into Furnace Street. Turn left at Bye Street (across from Betsie Lake) and follow signs to the park.

FURTHER INFORMATION: Village of Elberta, 151 Pearson, Elberta MI 49628 (231) 352-7201

BEACH FINDER

PARK NAME	DELORME	UNIVERSAL
Elberta Recreation Area	pg. 73, C5	map 10, C7

54 Frankfort Municipal Beach

The charming town of Frankfort maintains a municipal beach split by a long fishing pier and lighthouse. The south end has a small beach of soft, clean sand. This section is located in Frankfort Harbor and although there's a great view of boats cruising through the channel, the water tends to be on the murky side. The beach north of the pier is the one to visit. This generous section of beach is 360 feet deep, with Lake Michigan water that is remarkably clear and an incredible dune bluff to the north. Walk out on the pier for an unbeatable view of the bluff.

The entire beach measures about a half-mile in length. There's a wooden ramp that runs along the back of the north beach and extends to the pier, but the only restrooms are three sets of outhouses. Swing sets and volleyball nets are provided. The lifeguard stand was empty when we visited on July 3, but we were told that there is lifeguard service during busy summer weekends.

Parking can be tight, with a small lot off of Father Marquette Street behind the south section and 11 spaces off of Sac Street behind the north section, as well as some street parking. Both streets run off of Michigan Avenue from downtown Frankfort.

FEES: None

DIRECTIONS: M-22 into Frankfort to 7th Street. Follow the business district sign to Main Street. From Main, turn right

onto Michigan Avenue and park on either Sac Street or Fr. Marquette.

BEACH FINDER

PARK NAME	DELORME	UNIVERSAL
Frankfort Municipal Beach	pg. 73, C5	map 10, C7

FURTHER INFORMATION: City of Frankfort, 412 Main Street, Frankfort MI 49635 (231) 352-7117

55 Sleeping Bear Dunes National Lakeshore

Part of the National Park Service, the Sleeping Bear Dunes National Lakeshore encompasses more than 35 miles of Lake Michigan coastline. It offers scenes of unparalleled natural beauty, including magnificent beaches with sand dunes that tower as high as 460 feet above Lake Michigan.

Most famous is the Sleeping Bear dune itself, named from a Chippewa Indian legend about a mother bear and her two cubs who plunged into Lake Michigan to avoid a raging forest fire. As the legend continues, the mother bear finally made it to the opposite shore and climbed to the top of a bluff to wait for her babies. But the exhausted cubs drowned, and the faithful mother bear became the solitary dune overlooking the lake, while her cubs became the Manitou Islands.

Today the National Lakeshore offers fantastic views of the dunes on the Pierce Stocking Drive, a seven-mile route with marked nature points and overlooks. In addition to the dunes, the Lakeshore encompasses crystal clear lakes, quiet streams and dense beech-maple forests.

Recreational opportunities abound. Canoe down the Platte, Betsie or Crystal rivers or fish for coho and king salmon in the fall when the salmon return to the Platte to spawn. Take a ferry and visit the historic Manitou Islands. Hike the many trails through forests and meadows, or ski along the 50 miles of cross-country trails in winter. Hunt for deer, rabbit, turkey or waterfowl in season. Challenge your stamina on the famous dune climb or try walking the 3½-mile Dunes Trail.

Camping is available at the improved Platte River Campground or the primitive D.H. Day Campground, both of which are open from spring until fall on a first-come basis. The Platte River site offers a bathhouse with showers and some electrical hook-ups. D.H. Day provides water and vault toilets only. Stays at both campgrounds are limited to two weeks. Also available are group campsites near the Glen Lake Picnic Area and at the Platte River Campground. Backcountry campers can find sites on the mainland and on North and South Manitou islands. Backcountry camping permits are available at the Empire Visitors Center or at ranger stations.

A pass to the Lakeshore costs $7 per vehicle and is good for seven days. The park can be accessed from U.S.31 along Lake Michigan, U.S. 131 through Grand Rapids, or I-75, which runs the length of the state. The main road through the park is M-22, which connects to U.S. 31. A visitor center in Empire will introduce you to the Lakeshore. You can find out more about the park by calling (231) 326-5134, e-mailing slbe_nps.gov, checking the web at www.nps.gov/slbe, or writing the Sleeping Bear Dunes National Lakeshore, 9922 Front Street, Highway M-72,

Take a lazy ride down the Platte River and slowly drift into Lake Michigan's waves.

56 Lake Township Park and Platte River Point

The convergence of the Platte River with Lake Michigan, and the cooperation of Lake Township with the Sleeping Bear Dunes National Lakeshore combine to create one of the most unique, beautiful and just plain fun beaches in Michigan.

The warm, shallow Platte River flows lazily through Lake Township Park just before it empties into Lake Michigan. Its constant current creates a natural water ride, and swimmers on rafts, tubes, noodles or anything else that floats drift down the river, then bounce into Lake Michigan's waves.

The park, on the east side of the river, consists of a well-manicured lawn with picnic tables, grills, benches and a modern bathhouse. There's also a boat ramp but the shallow, rocky water is suitable primarily for canoes or kayaks. Walk north and you enter the Sleeping Bear Dunes Lakeshore, with a stony beach backed by dunes. Across the Platte River is a strip of rocky beach which opens to developing dunes and, on the other side of the dunes, a pristine Lake Michigan beach. The only way to access the beach on the Lake Michigan side is by wading or floating across the Platte. Beach shoes are a must.

The view of the Empire Bluffs and the Sleeping Bear is unparalleled. The area is a nesting site for the endangered piping plover, and two large areas of beach were roped off when we visited to

protect their habitat. The park also houses the landing site for Riverside Canoes, where boats and tubes can be rented (616-325-5622). Riverside is located just south of Lake Michigan Road. Boat liveries have been popular in this area since the turn of the century before there was road access, when picnickers would float down the river, then have their boats tied together and towed back by motor launch.

FEES: Donation box

DIRECTIONS: From Empire, take M-22 south to Lake Michigan Road. Turn west on Lake Michigan Road and take it to the end.

BEACH FINDER

PARK NAME	DELORME	UNIVERSAL
Lake Township Park / Platte River Point	pg. 73, C5	map 10, D6

FURTHER INFORMATION: Lake Township Park, Michigan Avenue, Honor MI 49640 (231) 325-5202

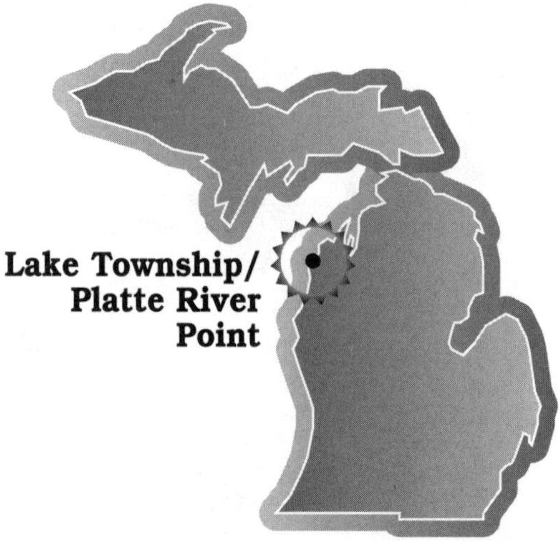

57 Peterson Beach

It's a long, bumpy ride on a dirt road off the beaten path, but this beach access in the Sleeping Bear Dunes is worth the trip. Located along Platte Bay, its beautiful vistas extend back to the parking area, which provide an expansive example of dune vegetation and wildflowers.

The long curving beach has delightful, soft sand and you can walk for miles along the bay. The swimming is unrestricted by ropes or buoys. Scanning the shoreline to the north, you can see the Sleeping Bear Dunes framed by South Manitou Island. To the south is a view of Platte River Point. A plank walkway leads over the low dunes to the beach. An outhouse and bike rack are provided, but parking is limited.

FEES: $7 for a seven day pass to the lakeshore

DIRECTIONS: North of Frankfort, take M-22 to Peterson Road, an unmarked dirt road across from Deadstream Road (about one mile north of Michigan Lake Road). Take the winding road north for 1.8 miles until it ends.

BEACH FINDER

PARK NAME	BEACH NAME	DELORME	UNIVERSAL
Sleeping Bear Dunes National Lakeshore	Peterson Beach	pg. 73, C6	map 10, D6

FURTHER INFORMATION: Sleeping Bear Dunes National Lakeshore, 9922 Front Street, Highway M-72, Empire MI 49630 (231) 326-5134

Peterson Beach

58 Esch Road Beach

Pull off M-22 at the south end of the Sleeping Bear Dunes National Lakeshore for a spectacularly scenic access to the coastline. Here the dunes pull back to form a small beach on the north shore of Platte Bay, with endless beachable coastline to the south. The view begs for a camera and the Lake Michigan surf is Caribbean blue, with a clean shoreline and open swimming. The sand is sugar fine, although littered with the remnants of evening campfires. An outhouse is the only facility provided.

Esch Road Beach is at the site of the vanished town of Aral, from 1880 to 1918 a thriving lumbering community. But once the forest was gone the town died out, and now only a commemorative sign remains to mark its heyday. The photograph on the cover of this book was taken at Esch Road Beach.

This one is a Beach Freaks "must" when visiting the Sleeping Bear Dunes.

FEES: $7 for a seven day pass to the lakeshore

DIRECTIONS: From Empire, take M-22 south to Esch Road. Head west on Esch Road until it ends.

BEACH FINDER

PARK NAME	BEACH NAME	DELORME	UNIVERSAL
Sleeping Bear Dunes National Lakeshore	Esch Road	pg. 73, B6	map 10, D6

Esch Road Beach looking north towards the Empire Bluffs.

FURTHER INFORMATION: Sleeping Bear Dunes National Lakeshore, 9922 Front Street, Highway M-72, Empire MI 49630 (231) 326-5134

Hunters of Petoskey stones scour the shoreline at Empire Beach.

59 Empire Beach

You literally have your choice of beaches in the village of Empire, in the Sleeping Bear Dunes National Lakeshore. The beach at South Bar Lake is just across the street from the town beach on Lake Michigan.

The local kids prefer the South Bar Lake Beach, which has a swimming dock and typically warm, calm inland lake water. There's also a small sandy beach, tables and grills and a nice playground.

Walk across to the Lake Michigan side to find a boat launch, bathhouse, covered shelter, playground, and volleyball and basketball courts. The beach itself is about ⅛ mile long and 50 to 100 feet deep. It's backed by a parking lot rather than dunes, but has scenic dune views to the north and south. Swimming is unrestricted by ropes or buoys. The sand is soft and pebbly, and here you can begin your search for Michigan's state stone, the Petoskey stone.

FEES: None

DIRECTIONS: M-22 to Front Street. West on Front to Lake Street. North (right) on Lake to Niagra Street. West (left) on Niagra to the beach.

BEACH FINDER

PARK NAME	DELORME	UNIVERSAL
Empire Beach	pg. 73, B6	map 45, D5

FURTHER INFORMATION: Village of Empire, 11518 LaCore Street, Empire MI 49630 (231) 326-5466

60 North Bar Lake Nature Preserve

This beach has been designated a protected Sleeping Bear Dunes nature preservation zone. Although recreational activities are encouraged, preservation and appreciation of natural features are its primary goal. Therefore, visitors are urged to respect the environment, stay off posted dune areas and leave behind no sign of their visit. Pets are not permitted and excessive noise from radios is discouraged.

You will, however, want to see this stunning beach, where serene North Bar Lake forms a channel that flows into Lake Michigan. Sunbathers can sit along the dunes on either lake. There is no longer boat access to North Bar, so quiet kayaks were all that disturbed its beauty. The beach stretches for miles on the Lake Michigan side with a stony shoreline, beautiful sand and splendid vistas. Swimming is fine in either lake, though cooler and rockier in Lake Michigan.

Getting to this beach takes some work, so don't attempt it if walking is problematic. There's a long walk from the parking lot, which offers an outhouse facility, to North Bar Lake. At North Bar a sandy path winds around the lake to the beaches. A wooden footpath traverses the dunes, or you can continue around the lake to the channel which leads to Lake Michigan. It's somewhat arduous, so prepare for a hike.

The North Bar Lake Nature Preserve is home to rare and endangered species such as the Pitcher's thistle, Michigan monkey flower, broom-rape and the prairie warbler. It is a lovely site,

Fragile dunes divide North Bar Lake on the left from Lake Michigan on the right.

recommended to those who will respect its fragile ecology.

FEES: $7 for a seven day pass to the lakeshore

DIRECTIONS: M-22 north from Empire to LaCore Road North. Take LaCore to Voice Road. Turn left on Voice and watch for a dirt road on the left. This is North Bar Lake Road, which may not be marked. Turn left and follow North Bar Lake Road to the end.

BEACH FINDER

PARK NAME	BEACH NAME	DELORME	UNIVERSAL
Sleeping Bear Dunes National Lakeshore	North Bar Lake Nature Preserve	pg. 73, B6	map 45, D5

FURTHER INFORMATION: Sleeping Bear Dunes National Lakeshore, 9922 Front Street, Highway M-72, Empire MI 49630 (231) 326-5134

Crystal blue waters of North Bar Lake.

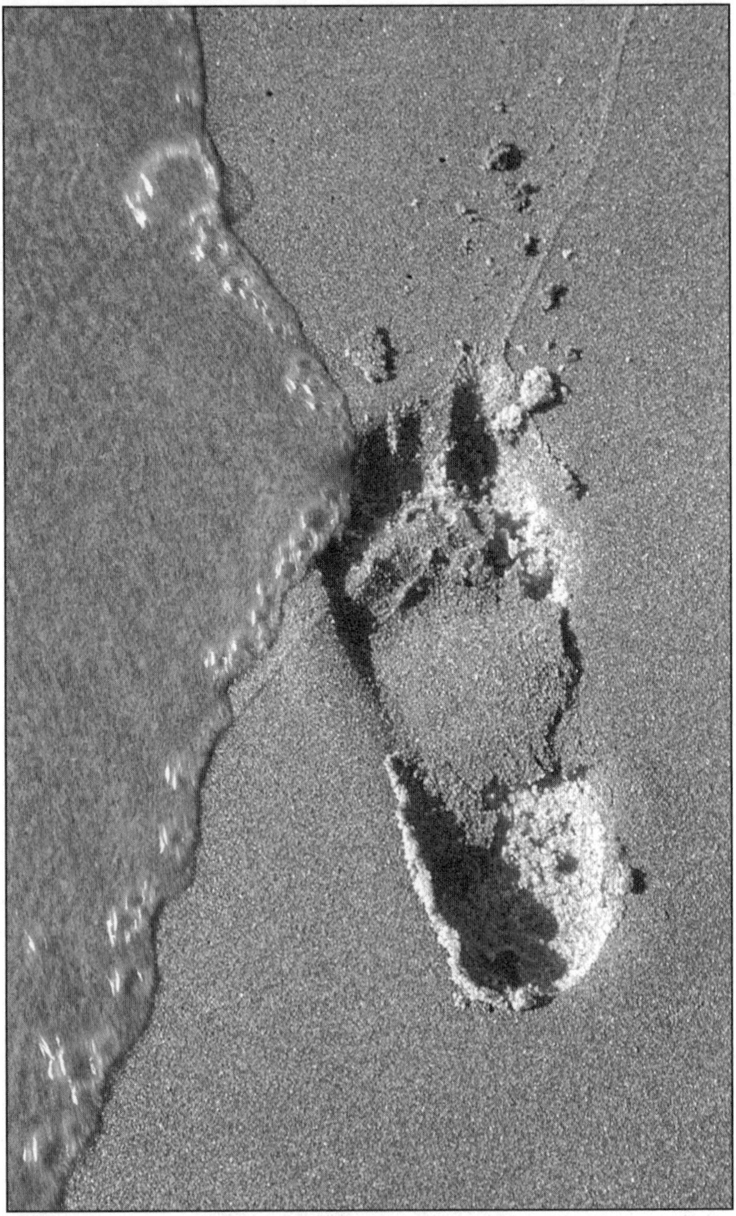

The black sands of Glen Haven beach can be found to some degree on almost all of the Great Lakes beaches.

61 Glen Haven Beach

The small collection of buildings at the end of M-109 in the Sleeping Bear Dunes National Lakeshore was once the thriving town of Glen Haven. A stopping place for steamboats and schooners traveling between Mackinaw City and Chicago, Glen Haven provided food, lodgings and supplies. Later a cannery was built and fruit was processed and shipped at Glen Haven's docks. Today several buildings, including the general store, Sleeping Bear Inn and the blacksmith's shop are in the process of being restored. The cannery is used to display boats and related artifacts of life on Lake Michigan. An example of a Great Lake fishing tug, the Aloha, stands on outdoor display.

Glen Haven is on Sleeping Bear Bay, and beach access is just behind the Glen Haven Canning Company building. The beach curves around the bay and has splendid views of both North and South Manitou islands. The beach is backed by dune grasses and is sprinkled with rocks, although the shoreline is clear and is great for a long stroll. The beach is narrow but is accessible all around the bay. An outhouse and a picnic area are provided.

Continue ½ mile south of Glen Haven to find the Maritime Museum. The museum is the remnant of a lifesaving station that was originally located at Sleeping Bear Point. The station, built in 1902, assisted the many ships that ran aground in the narrow Manitou passage. More than 80 wrecks occurred in the Sleeping Bear area. In 1931 shifting dunes threatened to bury the station, so it was moved by horses to its current location.

There is no additional fee to enter the museum.

Behind the museum is another access to the beach on Sleeping Bear Bay. Here the beach widens and flattens out, and the sand at the shoreline was heavy with the mineral magnatite, which produces black sand.

FEES: $7 for a seven day pass to the lakeshore

DIRECTIONS: M-22 to M-109 north to Glen Haven

BEACH FINDER

PARK NAME	BEACH NAME	DELORME	UNIVERSAL
Sleeping Bear Dunes	Glen Haven Beach	pg. 73, A6	map 45, E4

FURTHER INFORMATION: Sleeping Bear Dunes National Lakeshore, 9922 Front Street, Highway M-72, Empire MI 49630 (231) 326-5134

62 Good Harbor Bay Beach and Good Harbor Beach

Sparkling Good Harbor Bay lies just west of the Leelanau Peninsula in the Sleeping Bear Dunes National Lakeshore. Here you'll find two beach access points with miles of narrow coastline between them and lovely views of the dunes and North Manitou Island.

The more popular access is Good Harbor Beach, but both spots feature a narrow, sugar sand beach backed by developing dunes and the bluest water this side of the Bahamas. The shore is pebble-lined (watch for those Petoskeys) and the swimming is unrestricted by ropes or buoys. Swimmers should beware of old posts which may be underwater around the vicinity of the beach entrance. We spotted wild grapes growing off the parking area at Good Harbor Beach. Both areas have limited parking and provide outhouse facilities.

FEES: $7 for a seven day pass to the lakeshore

DIRECTIONS: From Leland, take M-22 south to Good Harbor Road (M-651), then west on Good Harbor Road to Good Harbor Beach. For Good Harbor Bay Beach, continue south on M-22 to Bohemian Road (M-669), then north on Bohemian to the beach.

FURTHER INFORMATION: Sleeping Bear Dunes National Lakeshore, 9922 Front Street, Highway M-72, Empire MI 49630 (231) 326-5134

BEACH FINDER

PARK NAME	BEACH NAME	DELORME	UNIVERSAL
Sleeping Bear Dunes National Lakeshore	Good Harbor Bay Beach	pg. 74, A1	map 45, F4
Sleeping Bear Dunes National Lakeshore	Good Harbor Beach	pg. 74, A1	map 45, F4

63 Leelanau State Park

The beach at Cathead Bay in Leelanau State Park is for dedicated Beach Freaks only, for it's a 1.2-mile hike through hills and forest to reach the shoreline. But the effort is rewarded with a splendid view of the tip of the Leelanau Peninsula to the east and Cathead Point to the west, and an unspoiled beach that curves around the entire length of the cove. The sugar sand is sprinkled with polished rocks, wood debris and seagull feathers. Swimmers have to endure about 10 feet of rocks before reaching the soft sand floor of the bay.

The bay water is blue, clear and wide open for swimming. Petoskey stones are hidden among the rocks at the water's edge, although they are not as plentiful as at some of the other beaches on the northwest shore of the state. The beach is backed by low dunes, shore grasses and woods. Pare down your gear to the bare essentials for the hike, and be sure to carry out whatever you bring with you. There are no trash receptacles or facilities on this natural beach.

Before visiting the beach, drive four miles up Woosley Lake Road to the state park campground, where a lighthouse built in 1916 guards Lighthouse Point at the tip of the little finger of the peninsula. You can tour the lighthouse and visit the museum for a $1 fee.

ABOUT THE PARK: This 1,300-acre state park is divided into two parcels separated by private land. The smaller section, at the tip of the peninsula, encompasses the lighthouse and museum, campground and day-use area. The larger parcel, around Cathead Bay and Lake Michigan, features dunes, marshes, wetlands and woodlands and is home to varied animal life and nesting birds. Birding opportunities abound in the early spring.

The 52-site rustic campground offers splendid views of the lake, and some sites are right on the rocky beach. The secluded campground is nestled in a densely wooded pine and cedar grove. Two mini-cabins with room to sleep four and a group site are also available. The day-use facility offers a grassy picnic area with tables, grills, a playground and a picnic shelter. About 8½ miles of hiking trails run through the park, and several of the loops are groomed for cross-country skiing.

FEES: Daily $4, Annual $20, Senior Citizen Annual $5

DIRECTIONS: From Traverse City, take M-22 north to M-201 North, which turns into County Road 629 (Woosley Lake Road). From Woosley Lake Road, turn left on Densmore Road (past the airport) to the entrance of the hiking trails and beach.

BEACH FINDER

PARK NAME	DELORME	UNIVERSAL
Leelanau State Park	pg. 80, C3	map 45, H1

FURTHER INFORMATION: Leelanau State Park, 15310 Lighthouse Point Road, Northport MI 49670 (231) 922-5270

64 Clinch Park

Next to Clinch Park on the shores of Grand Traverse Bay is a 1,500-foot, city-run beach with a lifeguard and good swimming. Its primary advantage is its proximity to the activities of Traverse City; its main drawback is its proximity to the traffic and noise of M-31, Traverse City's main thoroughfare.

The swim area is roped and buoyed, the water is clear and refreshing. The natural sand is a bit coarse but otherwise pleasant. A path behind the beach is used by rollerbladers, bikers and walkers and the marina next door provides plenty of boating activity.

Children will enjoy a visit to Clinch Park, where they can ride an old-fashioned three-car open kiddie train or peruse the 3½ -acre zoo, which specializes in exhibiting northern Michigan wildlife. The Con Foster Museum houses native American artifacts, arrowheads and pioneer collections. There are small fees for the museum, zoo and train.

Parking on the north side of Clinch Park is for the marina only. Park across M-31 in the metered lot and take the walkway under the road to the park and beach. A combination visit to the park and the beach makes a pleasant family outing.

FEES: None

DIRECTIONS: On M-31 North in downtown Traverse City, next to the Clinch Park Zoo and Con Foster Museum

BEACH FINDER

PARK NAME	DELORME	UNIVERSAL
Clinch Park	pg. 74, B2	map 28, H6

FURTHER INFORMATION: Clinch Park, Traverse City, 400 Boardman Avenue, Traverse City MI 49684 (231) 922-4904

65 Lighthouse Park

Welcome to the tip of the Old Mission Peninsula, where the crystal clear water and sugar sand beach call to all Beach Freaks. The beach at Lighthouse Park, nestled among hardwood trees and dune grass, is about 300 yards long at its center and can get crowded. Better to look for cars pulled off the road which leads to Lighthouse Park, between Merril Point and Old Mission Point. A short scramble down the rocks leads to a more secluded beaching experience along the shores of West Bay. Here the narrow beach is pristine and the crowds minimal. There are also several official pull-offs marked with park signs close to the park entrance, with room for a few cars each. These also lead to more secluded stretches of beach.

Swimming is difficult, since the bay is strewn with boulders large and small. But the water is crystal clear and the rocks are easy to spot, so bathers pick their way among them and wade into water so shallow that ½ mile from shore it's only hip deep. Bring a raft and float above the rocks. Beach shoes are essential.

The view is lovely, with the Leelanau Peninsula to the west and the shores of Antrim County to the east. Flocks of seagulls perch on the boulders which rise up from the bay.

Lighthouse Park is built around a picturesque 1870 lighthouse. The lighthouse cannot be toured, as it is now a private residence. A log cabin, built in 1858 and moved to the park in 1993, is being restored. There are a few tables and grills available, as well as three hiking trails and an outhouse.

This 1870 lighthouse lies on the 45th parallel, exactly halfway between the North Pole and the equator.

AN INTERESTING TIDBIT: The park lies on the 45th parallel, halfway between the North Pole and the equator.

FEES: None

DIRECTIONS: Follow M-37 North through the Old Mission Peninsula to the end.

BEACH FINDER

PARK NAME	DELORME	UNIVERSAL
Lighhouse Park	pg. 74, A4	map 28, J3

FURTHER INFORMATION: Peninsula Township Parks Dept., 13235 Center Road, Traverse City MI (231) 947-1120

66 Haserot Beach

Frustrated because the water is not swimmable at Mission Point? Travel south about three miles to charming Haserot Beach. Sandwiched between private shoreline, this ¼-mile long beach is worth noting for the amazing clarity of the water and the New England charm of the view - crystal blue water and sail-boats bobbing majestically at anchor. The sand is a mix of natural sugar sand and the coarser stony variety. The swim area is partially roped and buoyed. There is a lifeguard tower which was not staffed the August Friday that we visited.

A few tables and grills lie to the side on a grassy area, and a modern wooden climbing structure invites kids to play. At the end of the beach are a fishing dock, boat launch and swing set. Parking is in two small lots. An outhouse is available.

FEES: None

DIRECTIONS: From the tip of the old Mission Peninsula, take M-37 south about three miles to Swaney Road. Head east (left) on Swaney. The beach is on the right.

BEACH FINDER

PARK NAME	DELORME	UNIVERSAL
Haserot Beach	pg. 74, A4	map 28, J3

FURTHER INFORMATION: Peninsula Township Parks Dept., 13235 Center Road, Traverse City MI 49686 (231) 223-7322

Haserot Beach

67 Traverse City State Park

There's a whirlwind of activity around the beach at Traverse City State Park, located across the street from the park campground and accessible via a pedestrian overpass that crosses U.S. 31. You can rent hydroboats (glorified paddleboats) at the park, Jet Skis up the beach to the east, and bicycles at a stand near the Holiday Inn to the west. Across the street is an impressive miniature golf course.

The beach itself is a 700-foot strip of pure sugar sand on the east arm of Grand Traverse Bay. Only 60 feet wide, it does get crowded, as it is in the heart of Traverse City's hotel row. Behind the beach is a strip of lawn with tables and grills which opens to the parking lot, which is so conveniently close that some folks wheel out full-size gas grills from their campers for picnics. Busy U.S. 31 is right behind the parking area, but the crashing surf does a lot to drown out the noise of the road.

The swim area is buoyed but the limits aren't strictly enforced, as bathers swam anywhere they pleased on the day that we visited. The view of Old Mission Peninsula to the west and the beachfront hotels of Traverse City to the east is lovely. There is a bathhouse available with bathrooms and changing rooms.

ABOUT THE PARK: Looking for an inexpensive place to stay while visiting Traverse City? Reserve a spot well in advance at Traverse City State Park, which is only two miles from downtown. The park offers little more than 475 squeezed together campsites, one area of which is barrier-free. But with all of

Traverse City's activities at hand and a beautiful beach across the road, what more could you ask for?

FEES: Daily $4, Annual $20, Senior Citizen Annual $5

DIRECTIONS: U.S. 31 at 3 Mile Road in Traverse City

BEACH FINDER

PARK NAME	DELORME	UNIVERSAL
Traverse City State Park	pg. 74, B3	map 28, J6

FURTHER INFORMATION: Traverse City State Park, 1132 U.S. 31, Traverse City, MI 49684 (231) 947-7193

68 Elk Rapids Memorial Park

North of Traverse City in Elk Rapids is a pretty municipal park with good facilities and great swimming. Located in the east arm of Grand Traverse Bay, the water is warm and crystal clear. Elk Rapids' Municipal Harbor encloses the north side of the park and the Old Mission Peninsula wraps around the south side.

The beach is about 1,000 feet long and 100 feet deep with soft tan sand. A picnic area lies behind the beach. Provided are four well-maintained tennis courts, basketball and volleyball courts, a bike path and a modern children's playscape. All that is missing is a bathhouse, and two porta-johns have to suffice. Also displayed in the park is an 1874 school bell from the first high school in Elk Rapids.

FEES: None

DIRECTIONS: U.S. 31 to Elk Rapids. West on River Street through downtown to the park.

BEACH FINDER

PARK NAME	DELORME	UNIVERSAL
Elk Rapids Memorial Park	pg. 75, A4	map 5, A11

FURTHER INFORMATION: Elk Rapids Township Hall, 401 River Street, Elk Rapids MI 49629 (231) 264-9333

Elk Rapids
Memorial Park

69 Palmer-Wilcox-Gates Nature Preserve

No amenities

The Grand Traverse Regional Land Conservancy was established in 1991 to balance the growth occurring in northern Michigan with protection of significant natural land. The 15-acre Palmer-Wilcox-Gates Preserve, just north of Elk Rapids, is a glorious example of their work.

Park along the shoulder of Bayshore Drive and walk the short path through low dunes to the beach. A sign reminds you that this is not a public park and that you are a guest of the Conservancy. The shoreline on the east arm of Grand Traverse Bay curves to form a cove and looks out at Old Mission Peninsula. The beach is a narrow strip of soft sand backed by towering hemlocks, pine, fir and hardwoods.

The water is shallow and rocky, so bring your beach shoes. It is also crystal clear, so that rock-hunting involves only wading in and looking down. Because of its rockiness, this is really more of a wading beach than a swimming beach. Naturalists can spot rare wildflowers and birds along the edge of the dunes at this beautiful site.

FEES: None

DIRECTIONS: U.S. 31 in Elk Rapids to Bayshore Drive (at Ames and Dexter roads past the traffic light). Follow Bayshore for 1.8 miles. Park on the shoulder.

FURTHER INFORMATION: Grand Traverse Regional Land Conservancy, 624 Third Street, Traverse City MI 49681 (231) 929-7911

BEACH FINDER

PARK NAME	DELORME	UNIVERSAL
Palmer-Wilcox-Gates Nature Preserve	pg. 75, A4	map 5, A11

70 Barnes Park

Antrim County's Barnes Park in Eastport combines a popular campground with a picturesque Lake Michigan Beach.

The narrow beach forms a cove backed by heavily wooded low dunes. The fine sand is run through with stones and pebbles. The swimming is fine, although rocks continue for some distance on the lake floor until turning to soft sand, so beach shoes are advisable. The day of our visit found the lake choppy and rough, and swimmers were having a ball.

A wooden staircase leads down the bluffs from the parking area to the beach. The beach is integrated into the 76 site campground, which has both improved and unimproved wooded sites. Drive past the beach and around to the right to find the bathhouse (near campsite 15), which has restrooms and coin-operated showers. There's also a playground and two covered picnic shelters near the park entrance.

FEES: None to use the beach

DIRECTIONS: From Elk Rapids, north on U.S. 31 to Eastport. West on Barnes Park Road (at the junction with M-88) to the park

BEACH FINDER

PARK NAME	DELORME	UNIVERSAL
Barnes Park	pg. 81, D5	map 5, A9

FURTHER INFORMATION: Antrim County, 205 Cayuga, Bellaire MI 49615 (231) 533-8607

Barnes Park

71 Fisherman's Island State Park

A tunnel of trees that ends with a spectacular view of Lake Michigan marks the entrance of Fisherman's Island State Park, one of the least visited but most beautiful parks in Michigan. Fisherman's Island is a rock-hunter's dream. Its shores are composed of millions of rocks and stones, and Petoskey stones and excellent fossil specimens abound.

At the entrance of the park is a small parking area and access to an unspoiled beach. But spring for the $4 entrance fee and drive to the end of the main park road. There, a dirt parking lot leads to a path which takes you to a breathtakingly beautiful beach - unspoiled and secluded, with soft brown sand dotted with stones, gentle dunes and crashing Lake Michigan shoreline. You will see a phenomenal view of tiny Fisherman's Island, a 4.2-acre island just off the shore to the south which can actually be waded to if water conditions allow. Miles of gorgeous shoreline beg to be explored.

The only facilities near the beach are a couple of picnic tables and outhouses, so pack your own necessities. The park is divided into two sections separated by private property. This beach is in the northern section closer to Charlevoix.

ABOUT THE PARK: This 2,600-acre park, originally a limestone quarry, was given to the state forest system and named Bell's Bay State Forest Campground. Ownership eventually transferred to the DNR Parks Division, and the name changed in honor of the island.

Ninety wooded, rustic campsites are available, with some touching shoreline. The northern section of the park contains a five-mile hiking trail, while several unposted trails wind through the park's southern section. Hunters take grouse, deer, rabbits and fox, while fishing for steelhead and chinook salmon is popular at the park's two creeks.

The southern half of the park is undeveloped, and facilities are few in the northern half. Bring your own food and beverages and spend a day enjoying the spectacular natural beauty of Fisherman's Island.

FEES: Daily $4, Annual $20, Senior Citizen Annual $5

DIRECTIONS: From Charlevoix, drive five miles south on U.S. 31 to Bell's Bay Road. Turn right (west) on Bell's Bay Road and go 2.5 miles to the park entrance.

BEACH FINDER

PARK NAME	DELORME	UNIVERSAL
Fisherman's Island State Park	pg. 81, B5	map 15, A6

FURTHER INFORMATION: Fisherman's Island State Park, P.O. Box 456, Charlevoix MI 49720 (231) 547-6641

72 Michigan Beach

If you're looking for a good family beach in the Charlevoix area, Michigan Beach might be worth a visit. Located next to the Great Lakes Fisheries Station, this popular developed beach on Lake Michigan is close to downtown Charlevoix.

A protected swimming area with lifeguards eases worries about the little ones. The soft sand is strewn with rocks and stones, and Petoskey stone hunting is a popular pastime. A small pier and lighthouse can be walked to from the beach and there's a playground and picnic tables provided. Outhouses are the only restroom facilities. Unfortunately, the huge Medusa Concrete Plant detracts from the Lake Michigan view.

FEES: None

DIRECTIONS: From downtown Charlevoix, head west on Park Street to Grant Road, and right on Grant to the beach.

BEACH FINDER

PARK NAME	DELORME	UNIVERSAL
Michigan Beach	pg. 81, B5	map 15, A6

FURTHER INFORMATION: Charlevoix Recreation Dept., 210 State Street, Charlevoix MI 49720 (231) 547-3253

Michigan Beach

73 Mt. McSauba Recreation Area

No amenities

If it wasn't for the Medusa Concrete Plant towering above the lake directly in view (someone should disguise it as a dune), the spectacular Mt. McSauba Recreation Area would rate a top ten. For the rest of the view is gorgeous, with aquamarine water forming a cove and a clear view of Charlevoix to the south.

It's a bit of a sandy trudge from the parking area through dune bluffs which open on to a beautiful, wide beach with super fine, stone-free white sand. Backing the beach are irregularly-shaped dunes wooded with birch, beech and pine. Trails lead off of the path for exploring dune ecology. There are no amenities by the beach in this 52-acre park, just wonderful, open swimming and an endless, clean coastline to explore.

FEES: None

DIRECTIONS: From downtown Charlevoix at the bridge, take U.S. 31 north 1.1 miles to Mercer Blvd. Turn left on Mercer to Pleasant Street. Turn left on Pleasant to the park's parking lot.

BEACH FINDER

PARK NAME	DELORME	UNIVERSAL
Mt. McSauba Recreation Area	pg. 81, B5	map 15, A6

FURTHER INFORMATION: Charlevoix Recreation Department, 210 State Street, Charlevoix MI 49720 (231) 547-3253

74 Petoskey State Park

Minutes from Petoskey, Petoskey State Park is the place to go for sand, swimming and scenery. The 305-acre park offers a wide, almost mile-long beach with open dunes which are perfect for tucking your chair into on a windy day.

The soft beach is strewn with pebbles and its stony shore is popular for Petoskey stone hunting. Beach shoes will make walking a little easier. Swimming in Little Traverse Bay is buoyed but people were swimming all along the shore. There are great views of Petoskey wrapping around to the south and Harbor Springs to the north. There's a bathhouse with some tables available under an attached shelter, but no grilling is allowed. A playground is behind the parking lot and there's a volleyball net on the beach. It's a great natural beach with modern conveniences.

ABOUT THE PARK: One of the first owners of what is now park land was Pay-me-gwau, an Ottawa Indian who was deeded the property in an 1885 treaty. Many owners later, the City of Petoskey sold the Petoskey Bathing Beach to the state, and in 1969 Petoskey State Park was established.

The park is known for its 190-site, modern campground. The Dunes Campground has smaller sites edged by dunes, while the Tannery Creek Campground is better suited for trailers and RVs. A group camping site is also available. Three miles of hiking trails will lead you through the park, with the Old Baldy Trail climbing up the dunes for a panoramic view. The trails are maintained in the winter for cross-country skiing.

FEES: Daily $4, Annual $20, Senior Citizen Annual $5

DIRECTIONS: From Petoskey, take U.S. 31 about 3 miles to M-119. Turn left onto M-119 and follow the state park sign to the entrance.

BEACH FINDER

PARK NAME	DELORME	UNIVERSAL
Petoskey State Park	pg. 82, A1	map 24, D5

FURTHER INFORMATION: Petoskey State Park, 2475 Harbor Petoskey Road, Petoskey MI 49770 (231) 347-2311

◀*Featureless sun-bleached stones when dry, the Petoskey stones reveal their honeycomb pattern when wet. Petoskey stones and other fossils can be found along the shore at Petoskey State Park.*

75 Zorn Park Beach

This small city beach in Harbor Springs has more amenities than many larger venues. Right in the middle of the harbor with boats docked on either side, this stretch of soft sand has two swimming docks (one with a diving board), a nice play structure, a picnic area and a new bathhouse. The swimming area is buoyed and guarded.

The beach is only about 250 feet long and 50 feet deep, but the cool spring-fed water is exceptionally clear. As the only beach in town, it does draw a crowd.

FEES: None

DIRECTIONS: From downtown Harbor Springs, travel south on State Street to Bay Street. Go west (right) on Bay (it becomes one-way) to the beach.

BEACH FINDER

PARK NAME	DELORME	UNIVERSAL
Zorn Park Beach	pg. 82, A1	map 24, C5

FURTHER INFORMATION: Harbor Springs Parks Dept., 204 E. Fairview, Harbor Springs MI (231) 526-2091

Zorn Park Beach

76 Thorne Swift Nature Preserve

Although the public beach is small, the unique nature of the Thorne Swift Nature Preserve makes it worth a mention. Part of the Little Traverse Conservancy, this 30-acre preserve was opened in 1983 for preservation of shoreline, cedar swampland and dunes.

Visit the nature center before hitting the ¼-mile beach trail to the shore. There are three short, easy-to-walk trails which are all well-marked and maintained with boardwalk or wood chips. The trails, which pass through cedar swamps, evergreen woods and many varieties of wildflowers including the endangered Pitcher's thistle and Lake Huron tansy, are beautiful and the narrow shoreline is camera-ready. Boulders line the shore, and though swimming is possible bring your beach shoes to protect your feet. Of the 1,000-foot-long coastline in the preserve, 2/3 of it is protected and not open to foot traffic. However, a dune observation platform off the Balsam Trail has vistas of the coast. The nature center offers interpretive programs during the year.

FEES: $3 parking fee

DIRECTIONS: M-119 3.5 miles north of Harbor Springs. Watch for signs at Lower Shore Drive. Turn left on Lower Shore to the park.

BEACH FINDER

PARK NAME	DELORME	UNIVERSAL
Thorne Swift Nature Preserve	pg. 81, A7	map 24, C4

Thorne Swift
Nature Preserve

The beach on Sturgeon Bay tops the Beach Freak's list for its pristine beauty.

77 Wilderness State Park

Only a 12 mile drive from Mackinaw City lies Wilderness State Park, a Beach Freak's paradise of more than 30 miles of coastline on two bays at the western edge of the Straits of Mackinac. One of the lower peninsula's largest wilderness areas, the park shelters black bear, deer and bobcats, as well as an impressive array of birds and rare wildflowers. Modern campgrounds share the park with rustic cabins. Buy your fudge in Mackinaw City, but bring it to Wilderness for the ultimate high.

STURGEON BAY BEACH

Coming north up the Lake Michigan coastline from Cross Village, at the southern tip of Wilderness State Park is an awesomely beautiful beach on Sturgeon Bay. You'll see the dunes along the road; look for well-used paths over the dunes and roadside parking. Pull over and cross the wildflower-strewn dunes to find a pristine beach with jagged dunes, baby-soft sand and sparkling surf. The Lake Michigan water is clear and inviting, the sand soft brown and gently littered with stones. The view is breathtaking, with the uninhabited islands of Temperance and Waugoshance jutting off Waugoshance Point to the north, and Sturgeon Bay Point to the south. Crowds are few as there's miles of clear shoreline in which to spread out. The swimming is uncontrolled and superb. The day we visited found a section of beach roped off to protect nesting sites for the endangered piping plover. Outhouses are provided.

This end of the park is a Beach Freaks must. It's the last great beach on Michigan's beautiful northwest coast.

DIRECTIONS: From Cross Village, follow M-119 north. At Sturgeon Bay Trail, turn left. After about 1.5 miles of twisting road the terrain turns sandy and you'll spot a circular pull-off, or you can park at points along the shoulder for the next couple of miles.

BEACH FINDER

PARK NAME	BEACH NAME	DELORME	UNIVERSAL
Wilderness State Park	Sturgeon Bay Beach	pg. 94, C1	map 24, D2

BIG STONE BAY BEACH

The official swimming beach and picnic area near the campgrounds in Wilderness State Park, while not equaling the unspoiled beauty of the beach on Sturgeon Bay, is closer to Mackinaw City and definitely worth a visit. You'll find soft brown sand, great swimming and a pretty view of Laway's Settlement around the bay. Swimming buoys mark the water and a few picnic tables and grills are provided. Walk west along the shoreline to find a secluded spot.

ABOUT THE PARK: Two modern campgrounds with 250 sites share Wilderness State Park, the shady Pines Campground and the scenic Lakeshore Campground. Six rustic cabins on the beach may be rented, as may three large frontier cabins. More than 16 miles of trails are marked, from a short hike around a pond to an 11-mile loop through the back country.

There is a boat launch ramp west of the campgrounds and fishing is popular. Hunting is permitted in season, and the park is well-used in winter for camping, snowmobiling and cross-country skiing.

FEES: Daily $4, Annual $20, Senior Citizen Annual $5

DIRECTIONS: Twelve miles west of Mackinaw City on Wilderness Park Road.

BEACH FINDER

PARK NAME	BEACH NAME	DELORME	UNIVERSAL
Wilderness State Park	Big Stone Bay Beach	pg. 94, B1	map 24, D1

FURTHER INFORMATION: Wilderness State Park, Carp Lake MI 49718 (231) 436-5381

78 Lakeside Park

This lively local beach near Port Huron is popular with day trippers and boaters alike.

The 17 acre park provides a spacious, shaded lawn with tables and grills. The quarter-mile beach is about 90 feet wide. The natural sand is soft brown but is littered with stones that get progressively denser closer to shore. A gauntlet of rocks form a barrier into the clear blue water, so beach shoes are advisable for tender toes. Bring a beach umbrella to keep from roasting, as the rocks may prevent you from placing your chair close to the cooling surf.

The roped and buoyed swimming area runs the length of the beach, and doesn't get much more than five feet deep. Four lifeguard stands are staffed, weather permitting. Just outside the swim area, boats bob at anchor. The view is a peaceful contrast to the active beach, with sailboats in the distance and cruisers humming past. An occasional freighter steams by on its way into port.

Volleyball is the prime Lakeside sport, with two marked courts on the beach and two more, with bleachers for spectators, near the bathhouse. A play area contains traditional swings and slides as well as a brightly colored climbing structure. There are soft-drink machines but no concession stand provided.

One negative that must be noted was the poorly maintained restrooms which, on the date of our visit, had broken locks on the doors, broken faucets on the sinks and broken urinals in the men's room. The park facilities also were not handicapped accessible.

FEES: $1 for parking

DIRECTIONS: From downtown Port Huron north of the Blue Water Bridge, take M-25 north to Holland Street. Right on Holland to Gratiot, left on Gratiot to the park entrance. The park is between Holland and Krafft Street.

BEACH FINDER

PARK NAME	DELORME	UNIVERSAL
Lakeside Park	pg. 53, D7	map 74, L13

FURTHER INFORMATION: Lakeside Park, 3781 Lakeside Drive, Port Huron MI 48060 (810) 984-9760

79 Lexington Municipal Park

The lakeside city of Lexington, less than a half hour north of Port Huron, maintains an impressive facility on the shores of Lake Huron complete with a park, beach and marina.

The attractively landscaped park hosts special events such as concerts and art fairs. South of the park is the Lexington Mooring Facility, a public marina run by the city and the DNR. Wave runners may be rented in the marina and public restrooms are located in both the park and the marina. A walkway above a jetty runs alongside the marina, and is a popular spot for strolling and boat watching.

The lawn at the north end of the park has a smattering of tables and grills, and leads to a large beach. Unfortunately, the beach is large in the wrong dimensions. It is about 500 feet deep but only 100 feet across, so bathers are packed elbow-to-elbow by the shoreline. The unshaded depth of the beach does afford sun late into the day in spite of its east facing direction. The sand is soft, fine and pebble-strewn until the shoreline, where it turns coarser and has a thick band of stone leading into the water. The swimming area is not restricted by ropes or buoys but is small by default. The marina provides lots of boating and Jet Ski hubbub.

There is no concession stand in the park, but the city marina abuts a private marina which has a store and a small restaurant. A barrier-free ramp was built in 1994 providing handicapped access to the beach. A swing set is located on the lawn and a bright modern climbing structure sits on the beach. The pretty view, with the jetty and boat docks to the south and a sandy cove and two wooded points to the north, complete the picture. If only the beach were larger...

FEES: None

DIRECTIONS: From Main Street in downtown Lexington, take Simons Street east to the park entrance.

BEACH FINDER

PARK NAME	DELORME	UNIVERSAL
Lexington Municipal Park	pg. 53, B6	map 76, K10

FURTHER INFORMATION: Village of Lexington, 7227 Huron Street, Lexington MI 48450 (359) 8631

80 Lexington Park

It's unusual to see laundry flapping on a clothesline at a public park, but that's the sight that greeted us at this lightly used Sanilac County facility. The park manager's house sits squarely in the middle of the south section of the park, and her clothes were drying in the late June sun.

The park is divided into two halves by a wooden foot bridge. The south end has grills and picnic tables, a bathhouse and play equipment. The north end has tennis courts, a ball field, a horseshoe pit, a covered pavilion and additional picnic areas. Swings, slides and jungle gyms overlook the lake.

Three sets of steps angle down to a narrow, curving beach on Lake Huron. These rather steep steps are the only access to the beach. The beach extends roughly a third of a mile, with deciduous growth overhanging the fine, soft sand. The excellent quality sand turns into gravel and polished stone at the shoreline but the lake floor remains soft, the unguarded water sparkling blue.

Camping, which had been discontinued in the park, is offered again in 1999 with 42 sites for both RV's and tents. Hopefully campers won't overwhelm the narrow beach, which was sparsely populated in spite of the perfect summer weather on the day of our visit. The heavy woodlands behind the narrow beach provides for early evening shade, so come early in the day for the best tanning rays.

FEES: $2 donation, $10 annual

DIRECTIONS: Located on M-25, three miles north of Lexington just north of County Farm Road

BEACH FINDER

PARK NAME	DELORME	UNIVERSAL
Lexington Park	pg. 53, C6	map 76, K10

FURTHER INFORMATION: Sanilac County Parks, 2820 Lakeshore, Carsonville MI 48419 (810) 622-8715

81 Forester Park

Six miles north of Port Sanilac is Sanilac County's Forester Park, a campground and day-use area on Lake Huron. There's a rustic camp revival feeling to this park, and church and gospel groups are regular users. The day of our visit found an outdoor church service in progress on the lawn.

The park offers tables and grills, a recreation field, a sand volleyball court and half-court basketball. Playground equipment is scattered throughout the park. A store sells camping supplies, munchies, hand-dipped ice cream and even live bait. A video game room is in the same building. A covered pavilion can be rented, as can an enclosed pavilion for group use. Campers will find 171 grassy and shaded sites with electrical hookups and showers available.

Two long sets of steps or a sandy incline lead to a narrow ⅛-mile-long by 30- foot wide beach. The soft, fine sand is strewn with pebbles, wood debris and remnants of evening campfires. Vegetation and trees grow right up to the sand. As is typical of this area of coastline, a band of stones lines the shoreline and the entrance to the lake floor is rocky. This narrow beach gets crowded with campers and their little campettes, and the stones prevent a leisurely stroll along the shoreline. Tree growth causes sections of the beach to become shaded by mid-afternoon, so its best to arrive early.

FEES: $2 donation

DIRECTIONS: Located 6.5 miles north of Port Sanilac on M-25.

BEACH FINDER

PARK NAME	DELORME	UNIVERSAL
Forester Park	pg. 63, D6	map 76, K8

FURTHER INFORMATION: Sanilac County Parks, 2820 N. Lakeshore, Carsonville MI 48419 (810) 622-8715

82 Bird Creek Park

Port Austin, near the tip of Michigan's thumb, presents a well-maintained day- use area on Lake Huron called Bird Creek Park.

The long, narrow beach has fine, clean, yellow sand. The buoyed swimming area is unguarded and runs the length of the beach. The sandy lake floor is soft and free of rocks. A private firm rents paddleboats and aquacycles (water bicycles) as well as running a concession stand at the east end of the beach.

Behind the beach runs a scenic boardwalk with built-in benches and four sheltered overlooks, each housing a picnic table. The west end of the park has a rental pavilion and a playground featuring tire swings, slides, a wooden climbing structure and a unique wood and rope jungle gym. Behind the beach and boardwalk is an open picnic area with tables and grills but little shade. A state marina lies west of the park, and its harbor and jetty extending around Bird Creek Park make for a pretty view.

Amenities include two private showers, one of which is handicapped accessible. The boardwalk has ramps to the beach for accessibility.

FEES: None

DIRECTIONS: East from downtown Port Austin, turn right (north) on McMahon Street, left (west) on Farrar Street to the park.

BEACH FINDER

PARK NAME	DELORME	UNIVERSAL
Bird Creek Park	pg. 63, A6	map 32, G1

FURTHER INFORMATION: Port Austin, 393 Starboard Drive, Port Austin MI 48467 (517) 738-6808

A 1,000 foot boardwalk traverses the dunes at Port Crescent State Park

83 Port Crescent State Park

High water levels during our visit found a small beach at Port Crescent State Park, heading west from the tip of the Thumb on Lake Huron. This long beach nestled into a cove on Saginaw Bay consisted of strips of sand indented into surrounding grass and tree-covered dunes, with the dune grasses at some points coming almost to the water line. A park ranger informed us that the beach is usually twice as big, which wouldn't make it a spacious site but would certainly improve its usability.

Soft, fine sand slopes down to the Lake Huron shore which, to the delight of the children swimming, was warm and rough with waves. A buoyed "safe swim area" runs along part of the beach, but swimming is allowed all along the three-mile shoreline. From the parking lot, a path leads to a large rental picnic shelter which also houses the public restrooms. Cross over to the right side of the shelter to find a boardwalk which leads to the beach. This walkway isn't marked and may be a little confusing. Be sure to follow the path to the left with only one handrail - that's the path to the beach.

A thousand feet of boardwalk traverse the dunes, with five decks providing sites for picnics or scenic views. A cooperative effort between the state and the Audubon Society is providing another boardwalk and observation deck, which birdwatchers will be able to use for viewing birds of the marshes. The boardwalk and decks are wheelchair accessible, although the only access to the beach are stairways.

This north facing beach is the first of the beaches with a westward view from the tip of the thumb and is well worth a visit during the peak of the summer, especially when the water level is low.

ABOUT THE PARK: The main portion of this 565-acre park lies on the site of the old town of Port Crescent, which vanished around 1936. Part of the property also used to belong to the Ford Motor Company, which mined the fine sand for automotive glass.

Port Crescent offers 138 modern campsites, with some along the beach and old river channel. It also has a rustic organizational campground on an island bounded by the Pinnebog River and Lake Huron. A 2½-mile marked hiking and cross-country ski trail winds through the island.

The Pinnebog River offers stream fishing for perch, trout, salmon, smelt, pike and bass. Canoes may be launched from the park, or may be rented at Tip-A-Thumb Canoe (517-738-7656), on M-25 at the Pinnebog River Bridge. The day-use area includes picnic sites with grills, a 10-station fitness trail, and 3½ miles of marked hiking trails. Winter camping, ice fishing, snowmobiling and cross-country skiing are winter activities in the park. Candlelight cross-country ski runs are held several times during the winter.

FEES: Daily $4, Annual $20, Senior Citizen Annual $5

DIRECTIONS: Five miles west of Port Austin on M-25. The day-use entrance is two miles past the campground.

BEACH FINDER

PARK NAME	DELORME	UNIVERSAL
Port Crescent State Park	pg. 62, A2	map 32, F2

FURTHER INFORMATION: Port Crescent State Park, 1775 Port Austin Road, Port Austin MI 48467 (517) 738-8663

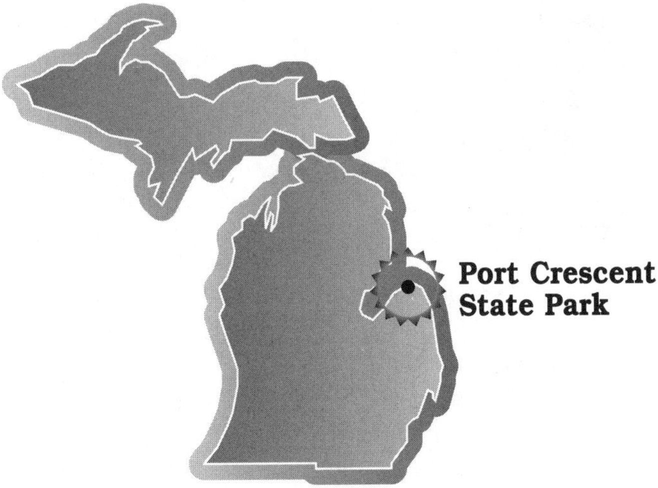
Port Crescent
State Park

84 Sleeper State Park

The beach at Sleeper State Park, four miles north of Caseville, has the silkiest sand on the Thumb, sugar-fine and clean.

There are numerous ways to access the beach from the parking lot - via an accessible concrete ramp from the bathhouse to the right, a sandy path to the left with a deck and a picnic overlook, a traditional stairway or a long, winding wooden boardwalk over the dunes. At the foot of these low dunes are wooden railings designed to keep people from climbing. It wasn't working, as enthusiastic kids were scrambling up and down the sand.

The half-mile-long beach provides plenty of room for sunning and strolling. The swimming on Saginaw Bay is fine, with a huge buoyed area that extends for much of the length of the beach. A rental shelter is available, and table and grills are located behind the parking lot. A covered stairway leads across M-25 from the beach to the park campground.

ABOUT THE PARK: Named for Albert E. Sleeper, governor of Michigan in 1916 and creator of the Michigan state park system, the park contains more than 700 acres, much of it undeveloped land providing hiking and ski trails, snowmobiling, and deer and small game hunting. The 280-site shaded campground provides electrical hookups and modern restroom and shower facilities. A large outdoor center features wilderness cabins, a kitchen and dining hall and a nature center. From the campground is the entrance to the Ridges Nature Trail, a self-guided trail identifying native trees, shrubs and wildflowers.

FEES: Daily $4, Annual $20, Senior Citizen Annual $5

DIRECTIONS: Located on M-25 four miles north of Caseville

BEACH FINDER

PARK NAME	DELORME	UNIVERSAL
Sleeper State Park	pg. 62, A1	map 32, E2

FURTHER INFORMATION: Sleeper State Park, 6573 State Park Road, Caseville MI 48725 (517) 856-4411

85 Caseville County Park

Huron County operates several parks with small beaches. The largest is in Caseville, in the upper west end of the thumb on Saginaw Bay. This complex, includes a modern 260-site campground across the road from the beach. It features a flat, open expanse of soft, fine, well-groomed sand that is remarkably fee of stones and plant debris. The long ⅛ mile by 200-foot beach abuts a large parking lot. A modern concession building also houses a sizable game room with up-to-date video games. Porta-Johns at either end of the beach supplement modern restrooms.

The buoyed swimming area is huge since the water remains shallow for hundreds of feet out. Boats cruise past a pier into a channel to the west or bob at anchor beyond the swim area. Two volleyball nets are located on the beach. This is not an outstanding site if you're looking for natural beauty, but its generous size, clean sand and enormous swimming area make it worth a look.

FEES: None

DIRECTIONS: From Caseville, head north on M-25 (Main Street in Caseville). Take County Road west from Main Street to the park entrance.

BEACH FINDER

PARK NAME	DELORME	UNIVERSAL
Caseville County Park	pg. 61, A7	map 32, D2

FURTHER INFORMATION: Huron County Sand Beach Division, 9 North Ruth Road, Harbor Beach MI 48441 (517) 479-3381

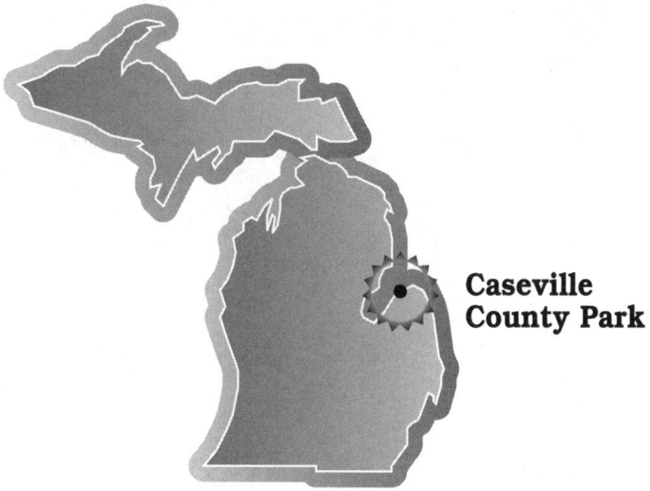

Kids love the animal sculptures at Tawas City Park.

86 Tawas City Park

One of the most popular vacation destinations on Michigan's eastern shore is the Tawas area, and the city park in downtown Tawas has one of the better beaches in the area. An art fair in the park drew a crowd on the early August day that we visited, and the beach was alive with young families.

The beach on Tawas Bay is split into two sections divided by a grassy pier that extends about 1,000 feet into the bay. The western section has two volleyball nets on the beach, the eastern section houses a small bathhouse. A concession stand sits at the end of the pier. The lighted pier could use a paint job, but is still

fine for sitting, strolling or fishing.

The beach 1,200 feet long by 100 feet deep, with soft, fine, natural sand. Picnic tables and grills are scattered about the beach and lawn and a covered pavilion with a large grill is available to rent. A gazebo is available on a first-come basis.

The bay water is refreshingly crisp and fairly clear, with a soft sand bottom and sandbars creating rolling waves. The buoyed swimming area extends 800 feet into the water so there's plenty of room to play.

Little kids will love the giant whale, hippo, shoe, fish, dog and especially the castle that they can climb in and on. For a city beach in the middle of town, Tawas Park rates a thumbs up.

FEES: None

DIRECTIONS: On U.S. 23 in downtown Tawas

BEACH FINDER

PARK NAME	DELORME	UNIVERSAL
Tawas City Park	pg. 71, B5	map 35, R7

FURTHER INFORMATION: Tawas City Park, 443 Lake Street, Tawas City MI 48763 (810) 984-9760

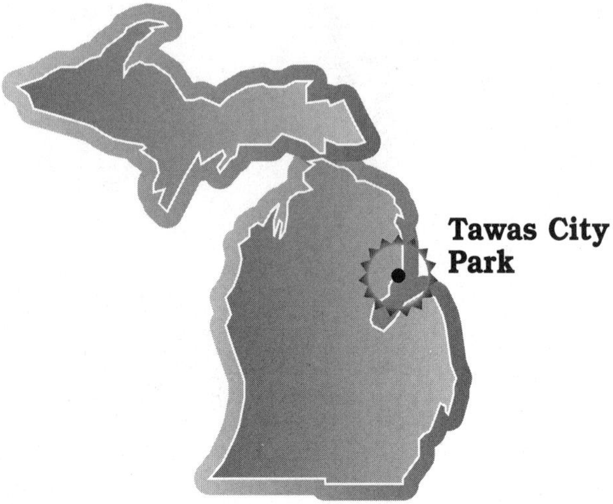

87 East Tawas City Park

Just down the road from the Tawas City Park is the East Tawas City Park, a full-facility park featuring a 170-site modern campground. This first-come first-served campground offers full hookups including cable television.

The 1,600-foot long beach is a narrow 20 feet deep, but offers the same soft sand and great swimming as its sister in the next town. Facilities in the park are outstanding, including an eye-popping wooden playscape for kids, a boat ramp, a rental gazebo that hosts evening concerts, picnic tables and grills on the lawn, and two horseshoe pits.

Modern restrooms are located in the park/campground office building. The park is next to the Iosco Historical Museum.

FEES: None

DIRECTIONS: On U.S. 23 in downtown East Tawas

BEACH FINDER

PARK NAME	DELORME	UNIVERSAL
East Tawas City Park	pg. 71, B6	map 35, R7

FURTHER INFORMATION: East Tawas City Park Commission, 407 W. Bay Street, East Tawas MI 48730 (517) 362-5562

East Tawas
City Park

88 Tawas Point State Park

Winding its way beside the limitless expanse of Lake Huron, the beach on Tawas Point offers soft sugar sand littered with bits of tree debris, gentle dunes and abundant plant and animal life. The popular beach is relatively narrow and does get crowded, but its meandering points and coves allow for privacy if you're willing to walk a bit.

If possible, you'll want to hike to the southern-most end of the beach, where Tawas Point forms a peninsular finger and creates the peaceful alcove of Tawas Bay. Boaters anchor and cast fishing lines into this gentle bay; plovers skitter and seagulls roost en masse by the interdunal ponds along the narrowing sliver of beach. Here vegetation grows almost into the lake. The constantly changing shoreline can make this route a challenge, but if the passage is open the ½ hour walk is worth the effort.

The clear Lake Huron water has broad sandbars that make it seem like you could wade into the water forever. Wooden scenic overlooks perch at the edge of the beach and a still operational 1876 lighthouse is available for touring on Friday, Saturday and Sunday during the summer.

ABOUT THE PARK: Calling itself the "Cape Cod of the Midwest," Tawas Point State Park hooks into Lake Huron to form Tawas Bay. A busy campground and day- use area, the 175-acre park is also an exceptional example of natural dune wetland ecology. The narrow shoreline at the peninsula's edge is constantly changed by weather and water, and natural vegetation and ani-

mal life abound. Birdwatching is a popular park activity, especially in the spring, as is fishing throughout the Tawas Bay area.

210 modern campsites are available for even the largest RVs, although the park does not provide a boat launch. A commercial marina close to the park entrance and a DNR boat ramp four miles away in East Tawas provide lake access.

FEES: Daily $4, Annual $20, Senior Citizen Annual $5

DIRECTIONS: East from U.S. 23, take Tawas Beach Road several miles into the park.

BEACH FINDER

PARK NAME	DELORME	UNIVERSAL
Tawas Point State Park	pg. 71, B6	map 35, R7

FURTHER INFORMATION: Tawas Point State Park, 686 Tawas Beach Road, East Tawas MI 48730 (517) 362-5041

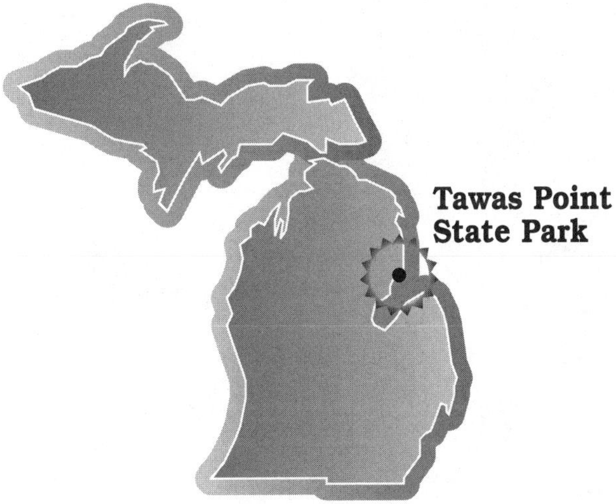

89 Roadside Park

Here's a beach that's easy to pass by, as it's noted only by a small brown sign off U.S. 23 about three miles north of Oscoda.

Naturalists will delight in this pristine wilderness beach of white "singing" sand, where dune grasses and wildflowers grow right up to the Lake Huron shore. Butterflies alight amid the milk-weed and purple thistle. The wavy surf is not monitored or buoyed, although locals report that the water rarely warms up before August. Pines and birch trees form a barrier between the beach and the two parking lots. A few tables and grills are available for picnics, and outhouses and two hand pumps are the only amenities provided.

The beach is more than a mile long and varies anywhere from a narrow strip to 100 feet to the tree line. Other than the unfortunate reminders of human occupation (old campfire ashes, cigarette butts and occasional litter), this rustic beach is a pleasant Beach Freak surprise.

FEES: None

DIRECTIONS: On U.S. 23, three miles north of Oscoda

BEACH FINDER

PARK NAME	DELORME	UNIVERSAL
Roadside Park (Three Mile)	pg. 71, A7	map 35, S5

FURTHER INFORMATION: Oscoda Township, 110 S. State Street, Oscoda MI 48750 (517) 739-4971

90 Oscoda Township Beach Park

A long lighted boardwalk overhung with trees and offering comfy benches is the outstanding feature of this nicely maintained township park. The winding walkway just behind the beach is ramped from the parking lot to the beach, making it handicapped accessible.

The beach consists of almost a half-mile of first-rate soft, fine sand sprinkled with wood debris. The crisp, clear, wavy surf has no buoys or other restrictions to swimming. Behind the boardwalk is lots of play space, including a colorful playscape, jungle gyms, swings and more. There's also a sand volleyball court, two full basketball courts, picnic tables, grills and a picnic shelter.

A bathhouse holds three showers as well as restrooms. There's no concession, so bring your own treats.

This is a pleasant place to spend the day!

FEES: None

DIRECTIONS: From Oscoda, take U.S. 23 (State Street) to River Road, then east on River Road two blocks to the park.

BEACH FINDER

PARK NAME	DELORME	UNIVERSAL
Oscoda Township Beach Park	pg. 71, A7	map 35, S6

FURTHER INFORMATION: Oscoda Township, 110 S. State Street, Oscoda MI 4750 (517) 739-4971

91 Harrisville State Park

A leisurely stroll along Lake Huron's shores is possible on the 2,750 feet of shoreline offered at Harrisville State Park. Bordered by a stand of pines and cedars and backed by wildflowers and vegetation, this is a delightful natural beach.

The day-use area just off the park entrance offers a picnic area with softball diamond, horseshoe pits, a basketball court and a volleyball court on the beach. Surprisingly, the restroom building is not handicapped accessible. A car-top boat launch and a rental picnic shelter are also close to the beach.

The soft, fine, tan sand is mixed with stones, especially at water's edge. Swimmers delight in the breaking waves in the buoyed swim area, which extends out about 150 feet. The beach width varies from 100 feet to 25 feet.

ABOUT THE PARK: Established in 1921, Harrisville is one of Michigan's oldest state parks. The 107-acre park offers 228 wooded campsites with modern restrooms and showers. Two mini-cabins which sleep four may be rented.

The two-mile Cedar Run guided nature trail, established in 1945, runs through forests of birch, ash, cedar and dogwood. Boating facilities for large craft are not available in the park, but a DNR access site is located in nearby Harrisville.

FEES: Daily $4, Annual $20, Senior Citizen Annual $5

DIRECTIONS: Located one mile south of Harrisville on U.S. 23, 1½ miles south of the M-72 intersection.

BEACH FINDER

PARK NAME	DELORME	UNIVERSAL
Harrisville State Park	pg. 79, C7	map 1, S3

FURTHER INFORMATION: Harrisville State Park, 248 State Park Road, P.O. Box 326, Harrisville MI 48740 (517) 724-5126

92 P.H. Hoeft State Park

Hoeft State Park has one of the prettiest picnic areas in the state. Located in a hardwood and conifer forest, each table and grill looks like its own little campsite. Even the old playground is tucked into the woods.

The beach access is not well-marked, almost as if the park wants to keep it undiscovered and uncrowded. From the park entrance, follow the "picnic area" signs. From the picnic parking lot, head to the south end (right) and follow the path and then the plank walkway over the low dunes to the beach.

Benches along the dunes let visitors enjoy the eastern view of almost solid horizon - from this vantage the sunrise would be spectacular. The narrow, mile-long beach is a rock hound's dream, strewn with rocks and excellent fossil samples. Despite the rocks, the sand is soft and the water swimmable, with a buoyed swim area and a stony shoreline.

A large picnic shelter/bathhouse built in the 1930's by the Civilian Conservation Corps is available for group rental.

ABOUT THE PARK: This 300-acre park is one of Michigan's oldest, donated to the state by lumber baron Paul H. Hoeft in 1922. The heavily wooded park has 144 modern, shaded campsites and an organizational campground. An improved mini-cabin that sleeps four can be rented. 4½ miles of trails run through the park and there's a bike trail that goes to Rogers City. Winter finds cross-country skiing and winter camping, with hunting permitted in half of the park.

FEES: Daily $4, Annual $20, Senior Citizen Annual $5

DIRECTIONS: On U.S. 23 four miles northwest of Rogers City

BEACH FINDER

PARK NAME	DELORME	UNIVERSAL
P.H. Hoeft State Park	pg. 84, A2	map 71, N4

FURTHER INFORMATION: P.H. Hoeft State Park, U.S. 23 North, Rogers City, MI 49779 (517) 734-2543

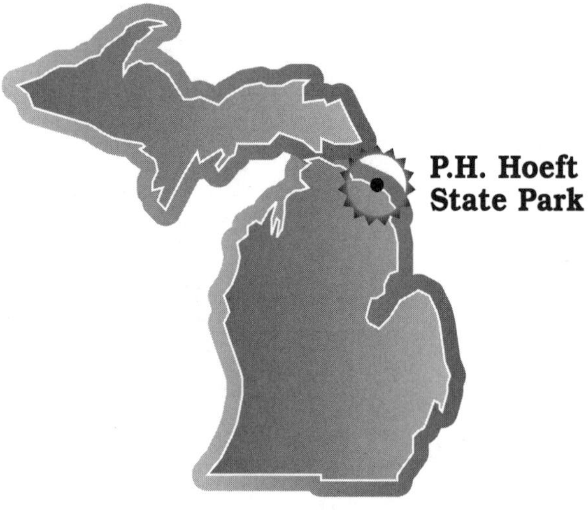

The northern view at Cheboygan State Park gives this beach a unique long distance look at the Mackinaw Bridge over Lake Huron.

93 Cheboygan State Park

That's the Mackinac Bridge in the distance as viewed from the north-facing beach at Cheboygan State Park. This lightly-used beach was almost empty at noon on a perfect July Saturday. And that's surprising, because the soft sand, 40-foot-deep and ¼-mile long beach is one of the best in northeast Michigan.

Located in Duncan Bay on Lake Huron, the child-friendly water was warm and shallow. Find a swale between the huge sandbars and take a dip in the exceptionally clear water. The flat beach is backed by irregular low dunes and pine woods.

The beach's facilities include a small playground, modern bath-house with an attached rental shelter and group-sized grill, and a picnic area. A concrete and wooden walkway leads from the parking lot to the beach. A pretty, wooded view around the bay completes the lovely picture.

ABOUT THE PARK: Originally a state forest campground, Cheboygan State Park now has 75 modern campsites. Three rustic family cabins and an organizational camp can also be rented. Five hiking trails run through woods and lakeshore. A launch for 14-to-16 foot boats provides bay access with great fishing for bass, northern pike and speckled brook trout in Little Billy Elliots Creek at the park's south end. The remains of the Cheboygan Point Lighthouse, built in 1859 and operational until 1930, can be seen by taking a dirt road to the north end of the park.

FEES: Daily $4, Annual $20, Senior Citizen Annual $5

DIRECTIONS: U.S. 23 about 3.5 miles south of Cheboygan

BEACH FINDER

PARK NAME	DELORME	UNIVERSAL
Cheboygan State Park	pg. 95, C5	map 16, H2

FURTHER INFORMATION: Cheboygan State Park, 4490 Beach Road, Cheboygan MI 49721 (616) 627-2811

94 Hiawatha National Forest

If you'd like to experience Lake Michigan from the Upper Peninsula, only 13 miles from the Mackinac Bridge is a nice stretch of coastline in the Hiawatha National Forest. You'll see the beach over low dunes from the road; a wide shoulder continuing for several miles allows you to pull over and park. You can then find a sandy path down the dunes or use one of a couple of sets of steps.

The west-facing, narrow beach offers miles of shoreline with soft tan sand and a clean coast for walking. Swimming is unrestricted by ropes or buoys and is terrific. The low dunes are grass and wildflower-covered and the lake view is of endless blue water. A lone volleyball net sat at the eastern end of the beach as the only amenity.

The Hiawatha National Forest covers much of the eastern half of the Upper Peninsula, and is bordered by lakes Superior, Huron and Michigan. The forest offers 22 campsites and miles of hiking and backpacking trails.

FEES: None

DIRECTIONS: 13 miles west on U.S. 2 from the Mackinac Bridge

BEACH FINDER

PARK NAME	DELORME	UNIVERSAL
Hiawatha National Forest	pg. 94, A1	map 49, na

FURTHER INFORMATION: Hiawatha National Forest, (906) 786-4062

95 U.S. 2 Rest Area

It's a long drive across the Upper Peninsula, but there's a pleasant surprise along its southern edge. Hidden behind a rest stop just east of Naubinway in Mackinac County is a pristine little beach.

This hidden jewel nestles against a newly built rest area, which features an attractive log cabin restroom building and a historical marker that details changes to this area's political boundaries. About a mile west of the stop is the northernmost point of Lake Michigan, which is noted as a Michigan Historic Site. This point was used to mark the western boundary of the territory of Michigan from 1805 to 1818. West of the line was Indiana Territory until 1818, when Michigan's boundary was pushed west to the Mississippi River and included all of the Upper Peninsula, along with what is now Wisconsin and part of Minnesota.

Two wooden walkways with picnic tables lead to a narrow, curving beach backed by woods and beach vegetation. The Lake Michigan water is crystal clear, shallow and inviting. This little beach makes a perfect place to stretch your legs and refresh your soul.

FEES: None

DIRECTIONS: Rest area off of U.S. 2, two miles east of Naubinway

BEACH FINDER

PARK NAME	DELORME	UNIVERSAL
U.S. 2 Rest Area	pg. 105, D5	map 49, na

FURTHER INFORMATION: Michigan Dept. of Transportation, (800) 654-8787

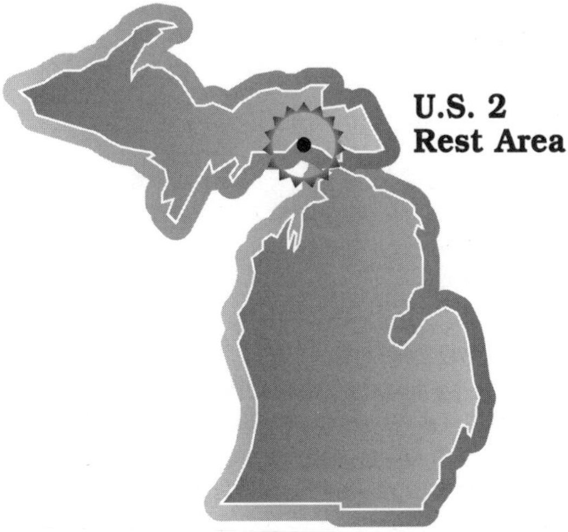

96 Rogers Park

A small park honoring Frank F. Rogers, Michigan's first elected highway commissioner who served from 1913 to 1929 and who laid out Michigan's first state highway system, can be found one mile east of Thompson in the U.P. Thompson is west of Manistique on U.S. 2.

The beach is only 25 feet wide (we were told it's often narrower according to lake levels), but it provides access to miles of shoreline. The spring-fed water is exceptionally clear and cool, and the sand is clean but damp from the springs. A flat picnic area with tables and grills lies behind the beach; unfortunately the proximity of the highway gives the park a rest area feel. Outhouses are provided.

Just west, look along the road for a tangle of downed trees, remnants of an intense storm that blew through the area in October 1997.

FEES: None

DIRECTIONS: On U.S. 2 between Manistique and Thompson.

BEACH FINDER

PARK NAME	DELORME	UNIVERSAL
Rogers Park	pg. 91, A6	map 77, na

FURTHER INFORMATION: Thompson Township Hall, Little Harbor Road, Manistique MI 49854 (906) 341-2441

Rogers Park

97 Brimley State Park

Our guidebook would not be complete unless we included a beach on that other big pond, Lake Superior. Close to Sault Ste. Marie and the Bay Mills Casino, Brimley State Park fits the bill.

Located along the shores of Whitefish Bay, the water temperature usually averages only 60 degrees, but the day of our visit found it warm enough for swimming despite the breezes that blew off the lake. The swimming area is buoyed and sandbar shallow, and bathers were jumping through waves that crashed beyond the buoy markers. The narrow beach is long enough to accommodate both campers and daily visitors with soft, fine sand and trees up to the beach line. The lovely view features land curving around the bay and freighters chugging toward the Soo Locks.

A large grassy picnic area affords plenty of space for activity and there's a volleyball net and playground on the lawn. The bathhouse has modern restrooms and although they are not handicapped accessible, there's a facility in the nearby campground that is. An enclosed rental picnic shelter is by the bathhouse. Brimley offers a good introduction to Lake Superior that isn't too far off the tourist track.

ABOUT THE PARK: Brimley is one of the upper peninsula's oldest parks, established in 1923. It features a 271-site modern campground and a mini-cabin with electricity. A boat launch provides access to Whitefish Bay and the St. Marys and Waiska rivers. Anglers will find perch, whitefish, bass, pike and walleye.

A stiff northern breeze kicks up waves at Whitefish Point on Lake Superior.

Hunting is permitted in season, and cross-country skiing and snowshoeing are the park's winter sports.

FEES: Daily $4, Annual $20, Senior Citizen Annual $5

DIRECTIONS: From I-75, take M-28 west to M-221. Turn right (north) through Brimley to 6 Mile Road. Turn right on 6 Mile and head east to the park.

BEACH FINDER

PARK NAME	DELORME	UNIVERSAL
Brimley State Park	pg. 106, A4	map 17, na

FURTHER INFORMATION: Brimley State Park, Rt. 2, Box 202, Brimley MI 49715 (906) 248-3422

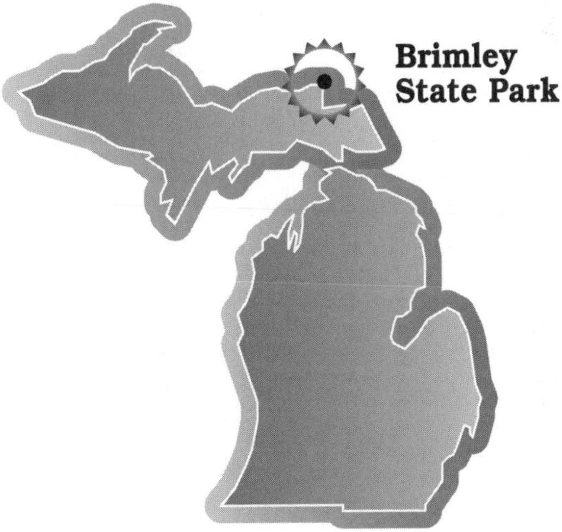

Bob Elmouchi at Tawas Point State Park in East Tawas. Right, Joan Elmouchi relaxes on the beach at Wilderness State Park in the city of Carp Lake

ABOUT THE AUTHORS

JOAN ELMOUCHI grew up two blocks from the beach in Atlantic City, N.J. and has felt a special connection with beaches ever since. A graduate of Rutgers University and the University of Michigan, she feels like a native after having lived in Michigan for almost 25 years. Joan is director of the Garden City Public Library and president of the Metro-Detroit Book and Author Society. Along with reading, gardening and country dancing, Joan's favorite pastime is lying in the sun on a Lake Michigan beach.

BOB ELMOUCHI is a native Michiganian. He has a degree in chemistry from Oakland University and was a commercial photographer for more than 20 years. Bob is now the environmental health and safety director for a major manufacturing company. An avid promoter of Michigan's beaches, Bob also enjoys singing, computers, photography and anything related to science. Bob and Joan live in Southfield, Michigan.

FRONT COVER - Esch Road Beach, Empire, Mi
BACK COVER - Bronson Park, Muskegon, Mi.

INDEX